The Handbook for Digital Printing and Variable-Data Printing

The Handbook for Digital Printing and Variable-Data Printing

by Penny K. Bennett, Ph.D.
with Harvey Robert Levenson, Ph.D.
and Frank J. Romano

Printing Industries Press
Pittsburgh

Library of Congress Catalog Card Number: 2006927738
International Standard Book Number: 0-88362-564-4,
978-0-88362-564-4

Printed in the United States of America

Printing Industries of America Catalog No. 1752
First Edition, September 2006

Printing Industries Press
Printing Industries of America
200 Deer Run Road
Sewickley, PA 15143-2600
Phone: 412-741-6860
Fax: 412-741-2311
Email: AWoodall@printing.org
Internet: www.printing.org/store

Orders to:
Online: www.printing.org/store
Phone: 800-910-4283 x770 or 412-259-1770
Fax: 412-749-9891
Email: membercentral@printing.org
Mail: Member Central, Printing Industries of America, 200 Deer Run Road, Sewickley, PA 15143

Contents

Dedication

I would like to dedicate this book to my two contributing authors, Harvey Levenson and Frank Romano. I have been very fortunate to be able to work with such outstanding individuals in the graphic communication industry. These two people share a love and dedication to this industry that is admirable. But what is even more admirable is their willingness to share their time and knowledge with anyone who asks. I thank them both for sharing their time and wisdom with me.

Harvey Levenson is not only my boss, but he is also my mentor and friend. I have worked with Harvey since coming to Cal Poly in 2000. He has helped mold me into being a leading educator in this country. He has encouraged and supported me while also sharing his strength and wisdom along the way. Thank you, Harvey!

Frank Romano was teaching two courses here at Cal Poly during the Winter 2006 quarter when I was writing this book. He offered early on to help me in any way he could. I was also fortunate that Frank's office was conveniently located right across the hall from mine on our campus. I would frequently go to Frank with a question regarding specific details pertinent to the subject matter. Frank was always there with openness and enthusiasm to share his knowledge with me. Thank you, Mr. Romano!

Preface

Our society at this very moment is in the middle of a digital revolution similar to the industrial revolution that we encountered in our society's earlier history. We are all watching our society change before our very eyes. We have moved rapidly from an analog era to a digital era. We have digitized text, images, and now audio and video. Digital data can be easily created, archived, retrieved, edited, and transported. We communicate in ways we couldn't before the digital world with the use of the Internet, email, and cell phones. We have consumer-driven hand-held devices that allow us to communicate via cell phone, email, or through Internet technology. Portable devices are combining together that also allow for GPS and MP3 options. Within a short period of time, one device will provide all our needs for use of all these technological options.

One main difference between the digital revolution and the industrial revolution is that no end appears in sight for digital evolution within the revolution. Technology improves, computing power increases astronomically, and it doesn't seem to have a definitive end. We are on this fast-moving technological train that doesn't seem to have a defined route or a defined destination. Regardless, it has changed the world we live in today. Technology has created an even faster paced society, and technology—specifically the Internet—has created a global market like we've never seen before. Ebay, for example, has become the most sophisticated world market available to the individual consumer.

It is important to recognize as we ride this technological train that the digital era has brought about diversification. Some analog processes such as analog photography will completely disappear. But many people reading this book will ask if digital printing will eventually replace traditional printing. My response is, "not likely in my lifetime." Print has and will shift from traditional to desktop printing to high production digital printing and various options in between. Print will diversify across various output options but the need for print to be distributed in a mass market form will continue. Just as podcasts will not replace mainstream television, digital printing will not entirely replace traditional printing. Both need to exist in our society today.

Acknowledgments

I would like to thank all the people in my life that have enabled me to write and produce this book. My children, Geoffrey and Eric, have been very patient and supportive with the time I've spent away from them during this time-consuming project. I love them very much and I thank them for their sacrifices. My friends Jeff, Barbara, Lonnie, and Robyn have all supported me in ways they have yet to fully understand. Thank you for your love and support along the way. Finally, I'd like to thank my parents, Bruce and Carol, who have always supported me in everything I've done and have always been there to let me know how proud they have been of me along the way. I love you both very much.

1. Introduction

EVOLUTION OF DIGITAL PRINTING

Digital printing is simply printing directly from a digital file. Digital printing has been available since Xerox developed the first laser printer in 1978. Various technologies and milestones since that time have contributed to the digital world we live in today.

Hewlett Packard (HP) introduced its LaserJet line in 1984. But probably more significant to our current use of technology is the development of desktop publishing. ***Desktop publishing*** became a reality in 1985 with the merging of three major contributors. Apple Computer developed the Macintosh computer in 1984 but found sales slowing in 1985. They then partnered with a newly formed company called Adobe and a small company called Aldus.

Adobe Systems, Inc. was formed in 1982 by two brilliant engineers, John Warnock and Charles Geschke. Warnock and Geschke had previously worked for the Xerox Corporation and developed a ***page-description language*** called "Interpress" that was used to control the Xerox laser printers. The two engineers tried to convince Xerox to make Interpress commercially available with a font technology based on vector outlines rather than bitmaps, but Xerox refused.

The name Adobe came from an Indian creek located behind John Warnock's house in Los Altos, California. The company initially contemplated developing a very powerful printer themselves but soon decided to develop print controllers for other printing manufacturers. The result was ***PostScript,*** which is a page-description language capable of driving ***laser printers*** to output high-quality text and graphics. Apple Computer became a natural partner for them.

Meanwhile, Apple Computer was developing a high-quality printing system known as the Apple LaserWriter. Aldus had already developed a ***page-layout program*** called ***PageMaker.*** With the use of PageMaker on the Macintosh for page design and the ability to output high-quality text and graphics on the ***Apple LaserWriter,*** desktop publishing was born.

The Apple LaserWriter initially sold for $7000. By today's standards this is a hefty price tag, but back then it was competing with the $500,000 price tag of the Xerox 9700 laser printer. For the first time in history, digital page creation and output of high-quality text and graphics became an affordable reality. The desktop publishing era was born and has evolved to the sophisticated digital publishing world we know today.

Digital printing presses can be defined as a high-speed option for outputting digital printing. The first digital presses debuted in 1993 at IPEX. They were the Indigo E-Print 1000 (figure 1-1) and the Xeikon DCP-1 (figure 1-2). The E-Print boasted the use of liquid ink while the DCP-1 used dry toner. Both presses represented the beginning of the digital press revolution. For the first time, we were experiencing a plateless printing press. Like any new technology, they were expensive to install and expensive to maintain.

The digital printer/press market has come a long way since 1993. Now there are over 11 vendors of digital presses including more than 24 different models. The quality and speed of digital presses have increased tremendously while the costs have continued to go down. Digital presses are available as both sheetfed and webfed, and most will print on a wide variety of substrates. Presses today have the capability to print using dry toner, liquid toner, or inkjet technology. The level of quality that can be reproduced on

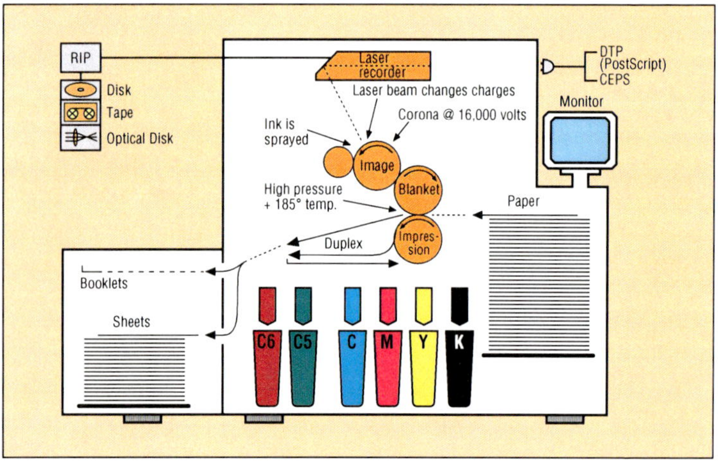

Figure 1-1. The basic operating principles of the Indigo E-Print 1000.

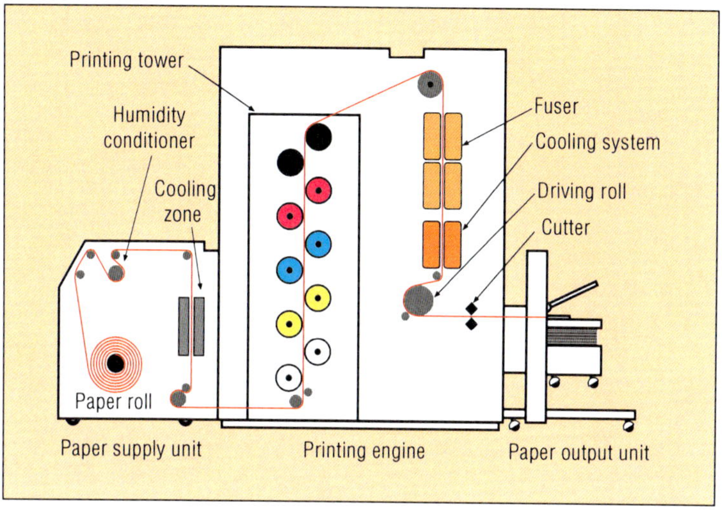

Figure 1-2. *General system schematic for the Xeikon DCP-1. Agfa sold its own version, the Chromapress, which was based on the Xeikon print engine.*

a digital press has reached and even surpassed the quality of print using some traditional printing methods. Digital presses will be discussed in more detail later.

EVOLUTION OF VARIABLE-DATA PRINTING

Variable-data printing (VDP) is simply the ability to vary data from page to page. The widespread use of personal computers with word processing and database capabilities in the 1980s really gave birth to VDP. Variable-data printing has been available even in the early days of Microsoft Word with its ability to do mail merge. The concept behind variable-data printing is to use certain static elements of information on a page and vary certain elements or information on the page to make it more customizable or personal. ***Mail merge*** allows text to be varied such as a person's name and address. The end result is to produce personalized form letters.

VDP has also been available for a long time in the form of direct mail. The ability to quickly put someone's name and address directly onto a mail piece has been available since the early to mid 1980s. As the PC platform began to develop during this time, affordable systems were becoming available for the mailing industry that could create the variable-data information and sort the mail for postal discounts. High-speed inkjet addressing capabilities began to come of age in the mid 1980s. Although databases had been around for a long time, it was also during the 1980s that database capabilities began to flourish. Affordable PC platforms allowed multiple users to enter and store data that could then be used for personalizing and addressing.

Since those early days, the level of sophistication for what can be varied has increased dramatically. Today there are several hundred software programs available for creating variable-data designs. Many have the ability to create varying text, graphics, charts, and even custom varying graphics. For example a person's name can be embedded into a picture, such as having his or her name written creatively into a beach photograph (figure 1-3). With the variety of options for software and digital printing engines, the trend in VDP color has also increased. Prior to full-color digital presses, there were many limitations on what elements could be varied. That is not the case today.

The trend has also shifted in recent years to provide variable digital data in the form of personalized web pages or personalized

Figure 1-3. *An example of a graphic image that has been customized by including the recipient's name in the image.*

emails. The evolution will continue but has been primarily driven by the increased capabilities of workflow, hardware, and software options. The number of people having not only Internet access but also high-speed Internet has shown astronomical growth. As this trend continues, it provides another media option for ***personalized marketing.***

INTRODUCTION TO DIGITAL PRINTING

Digital printing is simply printing directly from a digital file to a printed piece. Frank Romano, Professor Emeritus from RIT School of Print Media, defines ***digital printing*** as "any process that does not use a fixed-image and consumable image carrier (a plate)." Using this definition then, an image can be placed on a substrate through the use of spots or dots using a toner, inkjet, dye, or pigment-based transfer system. Digital printing can either be black-and-white or full-color. Full-color digital printing usually uses a combination of primary colors to create the full-color image. Some terms used to describe various forms of digital printing include ***short-run printing, on-demand printing, variable-data printing,*** and ***distribute-and-print.***

Digital-imaging (DI) press refers to a traditional printing press combined with technology that enables the image carrier to be imaged directly on the press. They are sometimes referred to as a hybrid system because they offer the traditional feed, delivery, and cylinder systems of a traditional offset press while also being able to image directly to press from a digital file. Usually a silicon-based material is used as the image carrier. An ablation process creates the image area allowing ink to adhere while the nonimage area remains smooth silicone to which the ink will not adhere. Therefore, they do not require a dampening system. Most DI presses use a waterless ink system. The digital file is processed through a RIP and the laser then images the dots or spots onto the plate material. Direct imaging presses are not capable of variable-data imaging, but they are well suited for medium- to short-run, full-color printing. Registration is very good and makeready is minimal as all colors are imaged precisely in place. Because of the precise registration, traditional prepress techniques such as trapping are not required. DI press manufacturers have included Heidelberg, Ryobi (figure 1-4), Scitex (now KBA), and Omni-Adast.

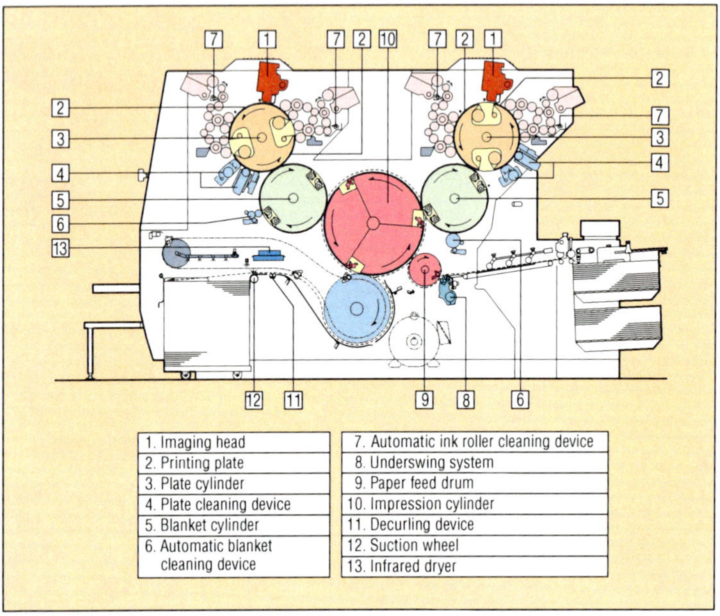

Figure 1-4. *The Ryobi 3404X-DI, a direct imaging press. (Courtesy Ryobi Limited)*

Digital presses can be differentiated from digital printers such as laser printers or desktop inkjet printers because of their ability to print at production speeds. Production speeds are generally measured in terms of pages per minute (ppm) or feet per minute (fpm) with webfed presses. Mid-level printers can be defined as printing 40–60 ppm. Production-level presses are generally defined as being able to produce 70 ppm or faster.

Digital presses other than DI presses can be categorized into either electrostatic printing or inkjet printing.

Electrophotographic, or ***electrostatic, digital presses*** start the imaging process by applying an electrostatic charge to the entire surface of a drum or belt. Next, the digital data allows a series of ***light-emitting diodes*** (LEDs) to eliminate the charge only in the nonimage areas of the drum or belt. Finally, ***toner*** is applied to the drum or belt and adheres only to the image areas. The toner also carries a charge allowing it to be attracted to the image areas. The toner is then transferred to a substrate and then fused onto the

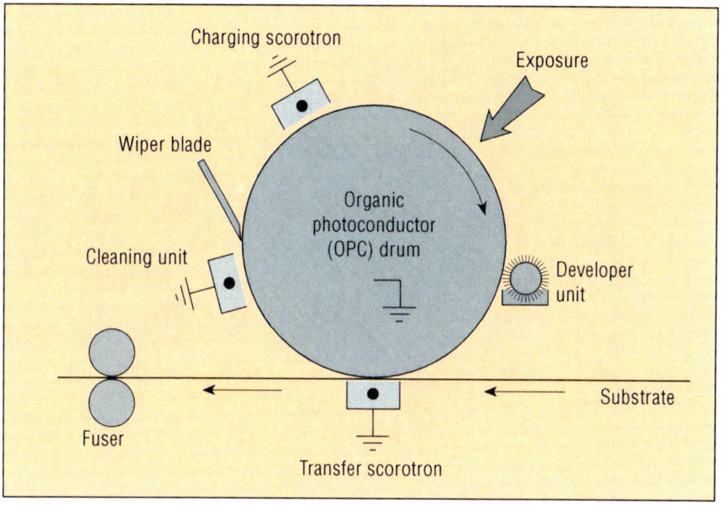

Figure 1-5. *The operating principle of an electrophotographic digital press.*

substrate using heat and pressure (figure 1-5). There are a wide variety of electrophotographic digital presses available from full-color to black-and-white only. Some are sheetfed while others are webfed. Most have the ability to print on a wide variety of substrates. Manufacturers include Xerox (figure 1-6), HP Indigo, Xeikon, Kodak, Konica, and Océ.

Inkjet digital presses are less common but will likely be an area of increased growth and market share in the digital press area. The overall growth in inkjet printing has been steady in

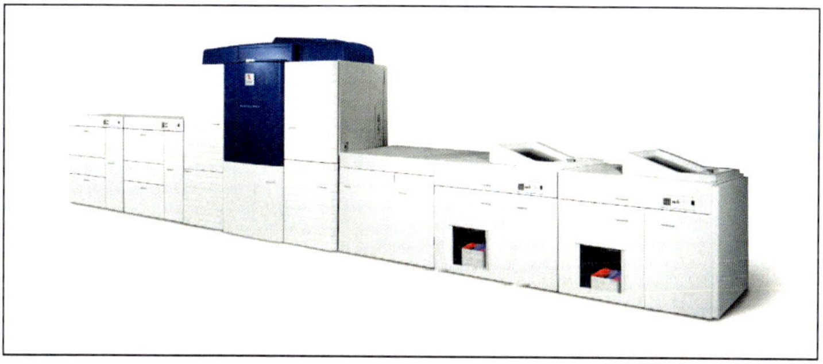

Figure 1-6. *Xerox iGen3™ 90/110 Digital Production Press. (Courtesy Xerox Corporation)*

every segment of the industry and will likely continue in the production-speed digital press area as well. Currently, two manufacturers make production-speed inkjet digital presses. The Agfa Dotrix produces very high-quality printing at high speeds on a variety of substrates. It does so with the use of an array of inkjet heads using drop-on-demand piezo technology (figure 1-7) and UV curable inks. Kodak's VersaMark is also a high-speed inkjet digital press using continuous inkjet print head technology (figure 1-8). Both presses use a webfed system for substrates. There has been a dramatic increase in the inkjet printers becoming available both in the desktop and proofing markets and also in the large-format markets including direct-to-signage and textile printing. It is likely that there will also be an increase in the available offerings for digital press inkjet technologies in the future.

On-demand printing is a term that came about with the development of production-speed digital presses. Printers have always produced jobs on demand as demanded by the customer, but the turnaround times for producing a job can be greatly reduced with the use of digital presses. On-demand printing can be printing from a quantity of one to a quantity of short to medium run lengths. ***On-demand publishing*** of books is a growing area. With the technology available using digital presses and binding capabilities, books can also be reproduced in small quantities of one or more in a matter of minutes. Publishers no longer have to worry about printing large quantities of books that may or may not sell. Books became out-of-print in the past due to low demand. On-demand book publishing can eliminate books from ever going out of print. The publisher only needs to worry about archiving a digital file of the book for reproduction as needed.

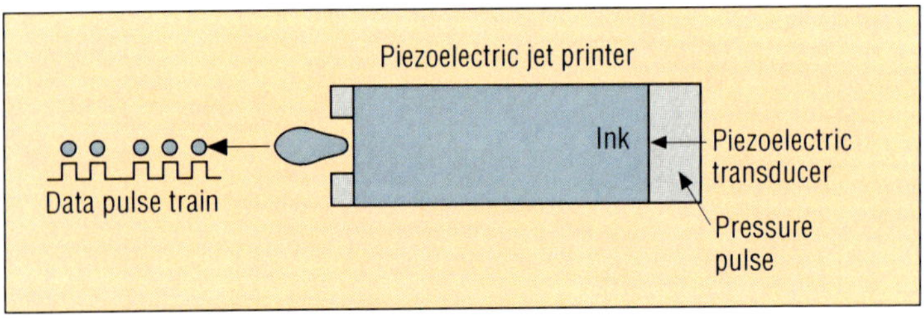

Figure 1-7. *Operating principle of piezoelectric drop-on-demand inkjet printer. (Courtesy PIRA International)*

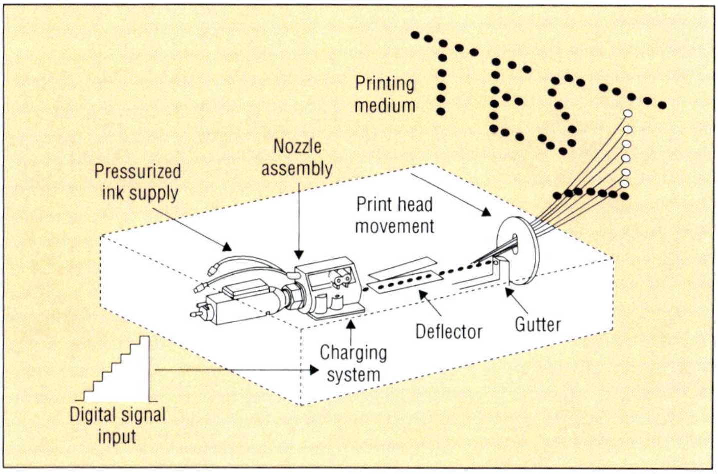

Figure 1-8. *Digital continuous inkjet. (Courtesy Marconi Data Systems, Inc.)*

Variable-data printing means that each printed piece can be different from each other. The amount of information that can change is quite vast. Most variable-data printing jobs are reproduced either all or in part on some type of production-level digital press. Other terms used for variable-data printing are ***personalized printing, customized printing,*** and ***one-to-one printing.*** Variable printing will be discussed in more detail later.

Distribute-and-print, another term used in conjunction with digital printing, is considered a form of on-demand printing. With the distribute-and-print workflow, digital files are created at a source location and then distributed to multiple locations where digital presses at each location print smaller quantities. The alternative to this workflow would be to print larger quantities of the job at a single location and then ship the printed job to various locations. The theory with distribute-and-print is that it would be faster—and possibly cheaper—to print at locations closer to the point of final delivery.

USES OF DIGITAL PRINTING

Digital printing has dramatically changed the way a printed document is reproduced. Most traditional printing today is reproduced using offset printing technology. Offset printing requires more time and makeready even with the latest computer-to-plate (CTP) technology. Digital printing requires no makeready and therefore can be used to run a quantity as small as one. Digital printing can be done using just black-and-white or color. Because of this, digital printing lends itself well to things like short-runs, custom publications, and personalized printing.

Short-Run

Short-run printing is generally considered the printing of quantities of less than 5000. Both digital press and offset presses are used for short-run printing, although the extensive makeready associated with offset presses usually makes it a less attractive alternative for short-run printing. As quantities increase, it becomes more cost-effective to use offset printing instead of digital printing. As digital presses increase in speed and consumables drop in price, however, the quantities considered to be short-run will increase.

Much of what is digitally printed today is considered short-run color with static images. In today's fast-paced society people want convenience, and they are willing to pay for it. Running a color job on a digital press can be accomplished much quicker than running a job using traditional printing methods. It is realistic and quite common for a customer to submit a PDF file to a printer and receive the printed job that same day or the next. The cost per printed piece will likely be higher than traditional printing, but if the quantities are lower, then the customer's overall cost is lower as well.

As digital presses have increased in speed and quality, there has been a continuous shift in jobs being run on digital presses rather than traditional presses. Most forecasts and trends show an increase in digital printing over time in both the amount of jobs being printed on digital presses and the increase in run lengths.

Custom Publication Printing

Digital printing has changed the way publishing is done. In the past, if a book or magazine was to be produced and distributed using offset printing, it was only cost-effective to reproduce large quantities of the publication because of the makeready time involved. With today's digital printing technology books and magazines can be reproduced in a quantity as small as one.

Because of this, there has been tremendous growth in the custom publication market.

On-demand publishing and self-publishing have flourished because of digital printing. Publishers can take in digital files directly from an author and easily create a relatively small number of publications. Books can be self-published and reproduced on a digital press. There are a variety of options for the binding of digitally reproduced publications including softcover, hardcover, and saddle-stitching. Binding can be done both in-line and off-line depending on the production workflow or quantity printed. The types of custom publications that can be done today are limited only by one's imagination.

VDP

Personalized printing is a type of variable-data printing. Personalized printing means that each page is distinctly different from the other. The only thing varying may be just a person's name or it may be the entire page. VDP means that the information on a page can vary but not necessarily on every page. VDP can include something like sale flyers printed for a large retail chain. There might be five different locations in which several flyers will be distributed for each store. The only thing that might change for each store will the store location, a street map, and the store hours. This is still considered VDP but is not considered personalized printing. VDP should be viewed as a type of digital printing. VDP actually represents a relatively small portion of the overall digital printing market. Most printers involved in producing variable-data printing have been involved five years or less. VDP requires more expertise and more time commitment for design and production whereas static digital printing can be reproduced relatively quickly. There are great opportunities for VDP as marketing trends shift towards more personalization.

2. Variable-Data Printing

WHAT IS VDP?

VDP can be viewed as either a tool for marketing or a production component of digital printing. From a marketing view, VDP is a form of personalized marketing, as shown in figure 2-1. Marketing can be categorized into mass marketing or personalized marketing. ***Mass marketing*** includes such things as TV/cable, Internet, newspaper, magazine, and various forms of signage such as billboards. ***Personalized marketing*** can be delivered in a variety of media forms such as printed (VDP), emails, or websites.

A term used to describe a marketing campaign incorporating various media for personalized marketing is referred to as ***cross-media personalized marketing.*** Marketers are realizing that personalization can help break through the marketing clutter associated with our society. Another term used is ***one-to-one marketing.*** The idea is to be more targeted with marketing and to send more relevant messages to a consumer. This concept will be discussed in chapter 11.

Personalized marketing can be delivered by sending an explicit message, a transparent message, or a combination of the two. ***Transparent personalization*** would be sending a message to an individual that is personally meant for them but they may not be aware of it. For example, a personalized marketing campaign could be developed for a group of people where the age of the person is known. Text and images can then be changed between specific age groups to appeal more to the age group being targeted. The person receiving the marketing message may not be aware that the information given to them may be different than information given to someone within another age group. ***Explicit personalization*** then would contain text or images specific to a given individual such as a person's name or business address. A marketing piece can contain both transparent and explicit messages.

VDP as it relates to marketing can then be categorized as either ***personalized*** or a form of ***versioning.*** A personalized piece would be designed to be unique for one specific person. A personalized document includes variations of text, graphics, and layout to

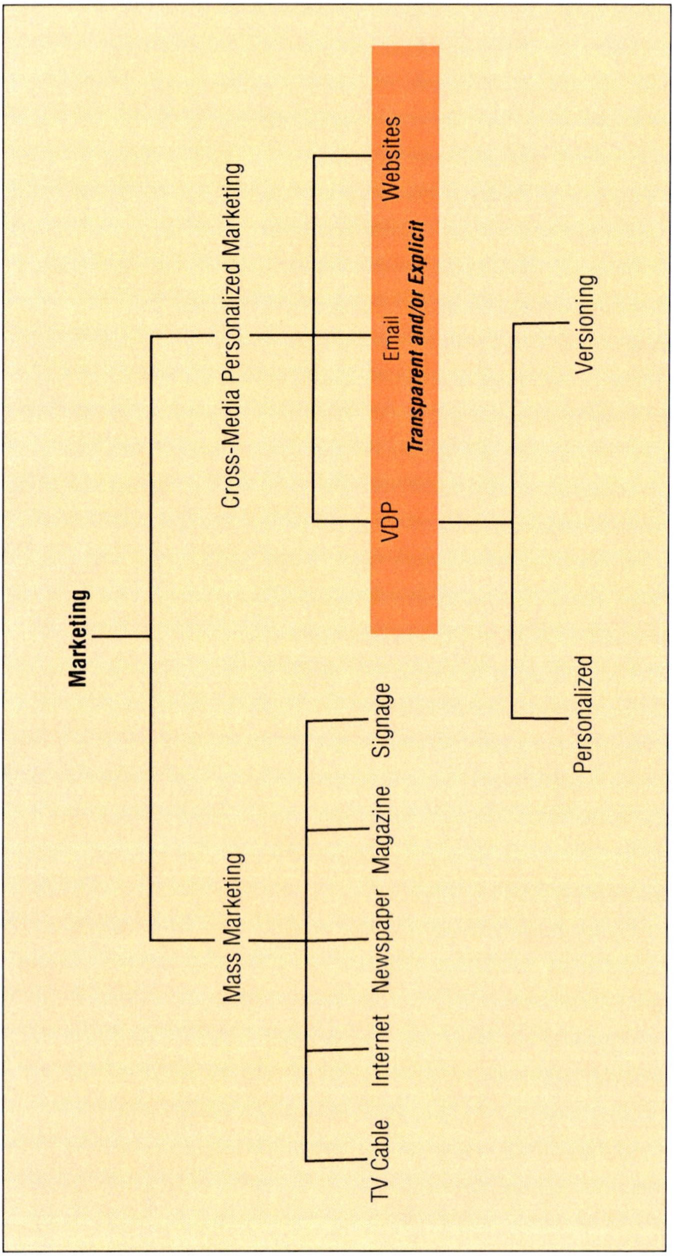

***Figure 2-1.** VDP as a component of marketing.*

meet the needs of an individual consumer. A common example would be a piece that has a person's first name built into the design and would therefore not be appropriate to send to any other individual. Versioning, on the other hand, can have the same design sent to multiple people. An example of versioning would be a printed piece listing a regional toll-free number or a mailer listing a local store location.

When viewing VDP as a production component of digital printing there are a few variances, as shown in figure 2-2. As previously mentioned, digital printing consists of short-run, VDP, and custom publication printing. In this view, VDP can either be reproduced for transactional or marketing purposes. VDP for marketing has already been discussed. Transactional printing includes all the bills and statements generated and sent to individuals or businesses. ***Transactional printing*** is printing of financial applications that incorporate personalized and customized content. Transactional printing is actually the single highest use of VDP today. Just like direct mail, transactional printing was one of the first forms of VDP and has been around for a long time.

As previously mentioned, VDP can take on many forms. The level and sophistication of how this can be done is quite diverse. VDP has been available for a long time in the form of direct mail.

Direct mail can simply be sending a mailing to a large group of people that only has their name and address on it. The varying elements on much of what we see in today's direct mail stream is black-and-white name and address changes only. This is really a form of mass marketing and is proven to be not as effective as more targeting marketing. VDP, then, is really a form of marketing.

Job Variations of VDP

Since the introduction of digital presses in 1993, the level of sophistication for designing and producing VDP has increased dramatically. With today's software, hardware, and digital printing engine capabilities, all elements of a printed piece can be varied in both color and black-and-white. As these tools have developed, there has continued to be more interest and growth in personalized marketing.

Variable-data printing can be achieved in a variety of ways and using a combination of different technologies to create a printed

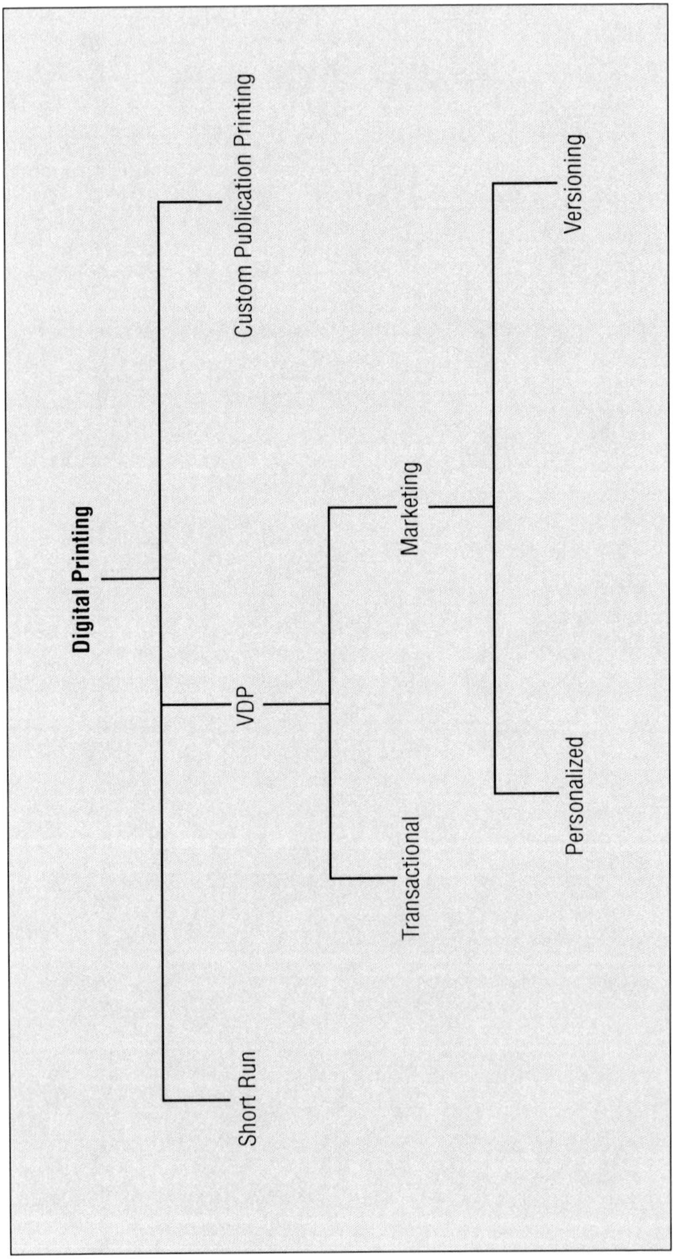

Figure 2-2. *VDP as a component of digital printing.*

piece. The elements involved in creating a variable-data piece are a series of static elements and a series of varying elements. Designs can include both text and graphics and can be just black-and-white or a combination of color with black-and-white. Some type of database must be used to incorporate the varying elements. With today's sophisticated software, virtually any element on the page can be varied, including graphics. In fact, everything on the page can change from sheet to sheet.

The equipment and technologies used to produce the finished product can be just as varied as the elements on the page. Production tools can include traditional printing presses, digital presses, inkjet mailing and addressing equipment, and even websites.

There are many ways and combinations of producing a VDP job. The job variations include the following:

- Preprinted shell
- Digital color press
- Digital black-and-white press
- Postpress
- Combination digital
- Transactional
- Versioning
- Web-to-print

Preprinted shell. One method of reproducing VDP is to preprint a colored "shell" of static information normally using traditional printing methods such as offset printing and then run the shell through a digital output device (e.g., high-speed black-and-white digital press, desktop laser printer, or inkjet printer) to add black-only varying elements to the preprinted piece. Usually, text and line graphics would be the varying elements added to the piece using this technology. This method is very common in VDP marketing. It can be a cost-effective way to generate a full-color variable-data piece when only black is required for the varying elements. If you think about it, most varying elements such as someone's name are text elements. Generally speaking, text reproduces better and is also more readable in black.

There are several advantages to using this method of reproduction. The big advantage is cost. A large number of shells can be preprinted and stored for use over time. For example, 24,000 colored pieces can be printed using offset printing. Then those preprinted shells could be imaged at the rate of 2,000 variable pieces per month from a digital black-and-white press for mailing. Offset printing still has advantages over digital printing, especially with toner-based systems. Cost-effectiveness over longer runs is an advantage of offset printing. Toner doesn't embed into the paper as well as offset ink and therefore can create issues of coverage or cracking of the finished piece. A preprinted offset shell resolves these issues nicely. For large quantities, it is by far the most cost-effective method of creating full-color VDP while still adding affordable black-only varying elements. One obvious disadvantage is the limitation on what elements can be varied within the piece.

Digital color press. VDP can also be produced today by outputting directly to a digital color press. The piece is produced entirely on a digital press in full color. Except for cutting, trimming, or folding, this method reproduces a completely digital variable-data piece ready to be mailed, such as that shown in figure 2-3.

Figure 2-3. *A digital color personalized, variable-data piece.*

Using this method, it is possible to vary every element on the page. Both text and graphics can be varied. Most of today's digital color presses have the ability to print on both sides of the sheet. The capabilities of what can be reproduced using digital color presses is almost limitless.

Although the flexibility of what can be varied is very good using this method, it is also important to understand that the more varying elements there are in a piece, the more complicated it can be to design and print. As the complexity of the piece goes up, so does the overall cost of the project.

Digital black-and-white press. Most digital press manufactures make a high-speed black-and-white press. VDP can be reproduced either partially or entirely on black-and-white digital presses. Although lack of color can put some limitations on the design, it can also be a faster and affordable way to create VDP.

Postpress. Until the development of digital color presses, variable-data printing was produced primarily by direct mail houses. Pieces printed on traditional printing equipment would go to the direct mail house to have primarily names and addresses added to the mailer. This method is similar to a preprinted shell, but the piece can be reproduced using offset printing or short-run color digital printing, depending on the quantity needed. The difference between this method and the preprinted shell is the equipment used to image the varying elements. In postpress operations, specialized high-speed addressing equipment has traditionally been used to address and perhaps add very limited varying elements of black only to the piece. Black-and-white high-speed inkjet, and sometimes laser technology, is generally used. Because of the historical use in mailing houses, the equipment and associated software is also efficient at addressing. It can image a printed piece with both addressing and postal requirements that help in the cost and efficiency of bulk mailing. This still represents a very large market of VDP today. It is quick and efficient and one of the most economical ways to market by mail. Because of the lack of ability for more personalization, it isn't considered the most effective type of VDP. If there is no other variation other than the addressing on the printed piece, this method is more likely considered a form of mass marketing than personalized marketing.

Combination digital. A variable-data printed piece produced using combination digital would include something partially created on a digital color press and then imaged again using another type of black-and-white press. The colored elements might be static for speed and efficiency and then varying elements such as black text may be added using a black-and-white digital press.

The advantage of using this method is that it can be more cost-effective from both a consumable usage vantage point and a time-efficiency vantage point. Consumables for digital color presses are generally higher than consumables for digital black-and-white presses. Planning a design that includes variation of only black-and-white elements can be less time consuming than planning and designing a more complicated piece. Obviously, if "click" charges are associated with both digital presses being used, this would not be a very cost-effective method to use. Another disadvantage of this method can be the substrate's ability or inability to withstand two passes of high heat associated with toner-based systems. Excessive curling and other quality-related issues could become a problem.

Transactional. Transactional printing includes the creation of financial documents such as bills, statements, or financial reports. Millions of bills and statements are printed worldwide. Most of these consist of primarily black-and-white digital printing on a preprinted shell. Transactional printing requires very high-speed production because of the volume generated. Transactional printing also requires a very quick turnaround time due to the time sensitivity of the information being printed. Many transactional printing presses are webfed because they offer much higher speeds than sheetfed and therefore faster turnaround for delivery.

Like most types of digital printing, transactional printing is changing and growing in complexity as the technology allows for more sophistication. As more people turn to bill paying on the Internet, transactional printers are looking to offer more services to their customers. Transactional printers are including more charts, graphs, and color into printed pieces as the speed and quality of digital presses improve.

Versioning. Versioning is the printing of different versions of a message designed to send a specific message to a specific group. Versioning can be a type of short-run printing using digital presses, or versioning can be done using conventional printing with a variety of messages being printed on a multiple-up press sheet. In versioning, different groups receive a different message. An example of versioning can be concert passes printed for various groups such as staff, security, and back-stage (figure 2-4). Versioning can be marketing related but in the example used above, it can be used in areas other than marketing. Versioning represents a very large segment of what is printed using VDP.

Figure 2-4. An example of versioning. (Courtesy Black Cat Entertainment)

Web-to-print. As more people gain access to the Internet, another method of variable-data printing creation is with the use of a web-enabled interface. Using this method, there is generally a template or series of elements that can be chosen by the user to create a design right within a given website. An example of a company that offers this method is Saepio Technologies, Inc. The user generally has several options from a choice of background to being able to add their own logo or dealer information, as shown in figure 2-5.

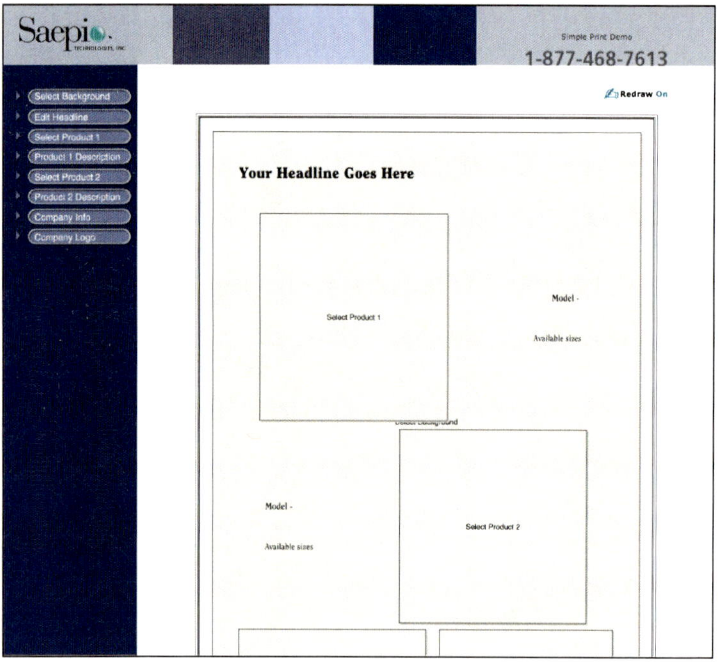

Figure 2-5. A template that allows the user to create a design within a given website. (Courtesy Saepio Technologies, Inc.)

Some interfaces even allow the user to upload their own database to finalize the personalization of the varying elements. When the design is completed (see figure 2-6), the user usually has the option to send the design directly to the printer or download the digital file in the form of an EPS or PDF file directly to their own computer.

Figure 2-6. A completed design, which can be sent directly to the printer or downloaded as an EPS or PDF file. (Courtesy Saepio Technologies, Inc.)

VDP PLANNING

It is important when planning for VDP that the most efficient and the most cost-effective method is used. This will depend largely on the existing equipment within a company, the quantity to be produced, the amount of variable information built into the design and the time to production. If a company has one full-color traditional press and one black-and-white digital press, then the options are limited. If the company has one full-color digital press and one black-and-white digital press, they may want to consider outsourcing colored preprinted shells for large-quantity jobs. If the press vendor charges per click versus per consumables, this could affect the overall decision. If large amounts of both colored and black-and-white variable information are built into a design, a digital press is the only choice. Depending on the quantity and design, versioning can be done on either a traditional press or a digital press.

3. Software for Variable-Data Printing

OVERVIEW

Designing for variable-data printing can involve a variety of software applications. The initial design of non-variable or static information is generally done in a page-layout program such as Adobe InDesign or QuarkXPress. Graphics software such as Adobe Illustrator and Adobe Photoshop can also be used in conjunction with the page-layout program for the initial design. Some type of database is used to collect and manage the data. Finally, a software program is needed to merge the static information together with the variable data.

Page layout. Popular page-layout programs such as Adobe InDesign and QuarkXPress (figure 3-1) are used for general layout and design of a printed piece. Microsoft Word and other less sophisticated layout programs can be used but are not recom-

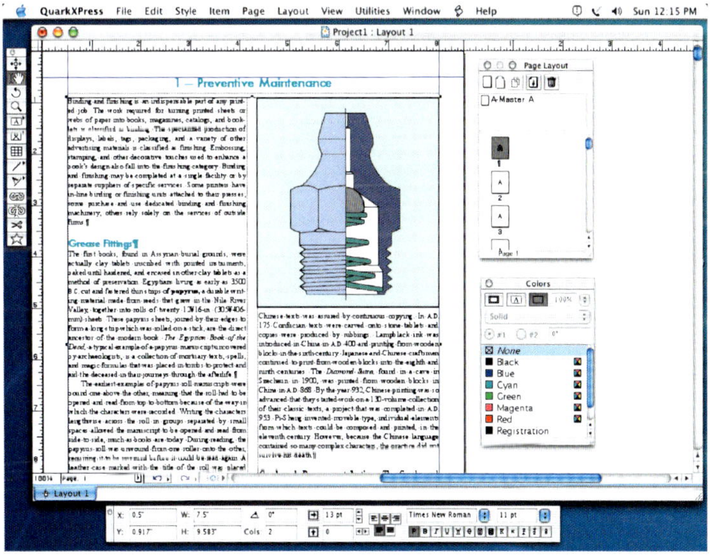

Figure 3-1. A page layout using QuarkXPress.

mended for professional designs. Quark and InDesign are much better for handling the graphic file formats and typographical requirements needed for professional design. Most VDP software also works quite well with these well-established programs.

The static parts of the design are created directly in the page-layout program. Page-layout programs are ideal for assembling of both text and graphics. They work well for any document size. It is best to plan the document size according to the finished printed size for VDP. Most VDP applications will not work well with a manually imposed or multiple-up documents built in a page-layout program. This would be better managed at the digital front end of the workflow.

Graphics. Graphics used for VDP layouts can either be static or variable. Regardless, the graphics creation and formatting process will not change. There are two major types of graphic files. ***Vector graphics*** are used for illustration or logo type work, while ***raster graphics*** are used for photo or graphics needing a large tonal value. The two predominant software programs used for graphics creation and editing are Adobe Illustrator and Adobe Photoshop. Illustrator (figure 5-3) works primarily with vector graphics while Photoshop

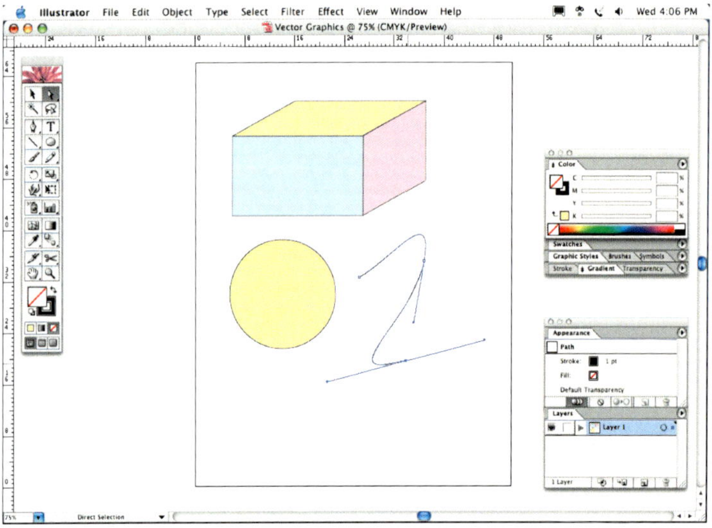

Figure 3-2. *Creating a vector graphic in Adobe Illustrator.*

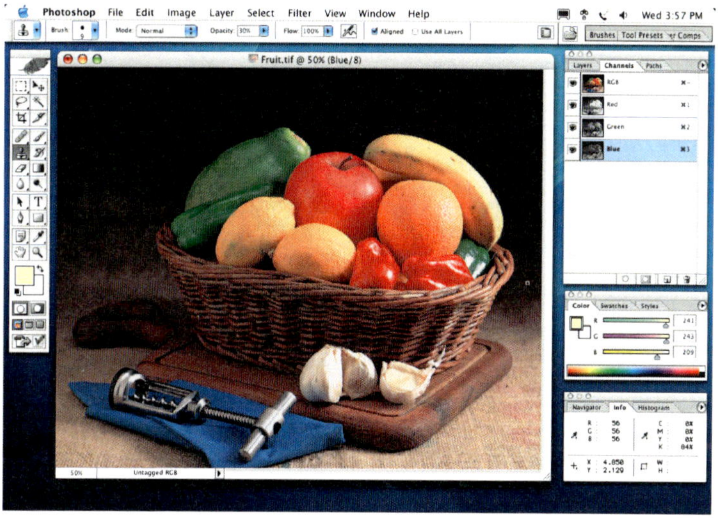

Figure 3-3. *Image editing with Adobe Photoshop.*

(figure 5-4) works primarily with raster graphics. Common file formats used in printing, including digital printing, are EPS files saved out of Illustrator and TIFF files saved out of Photoshop. Graphics and file formats will be discussed in greater detail in chapter 5.

Database. Data can be created and managed using any program that can save or export a data file compatible with the VDP software. Microsoft Excel can be used as well as FileMaker Pro, Microsoft Access, or any other compatible data management application. Database software and systems range from lower-end options like those mentioned above to more robust server-based systems such as SQL Server or Oracle. The choice in databases to use will depend primarily on the size of the database file and the level of sophistication needed for managing and manipulating the data. Databases will be discussed in more detail in chapter 10.

VDP SOFTWARE

Today there are hundreds of software options for designing and producing VDP. Software specifically designed to incorporate variable data into a design can be classified into one of two main categories: ***workstation-based applications*** and ***Web-to-print applications.*** Workstation-based applications can be further categorized into the following:

- Image personalization
- Stand-alone
- Plug-in
- Dynamic Layout
- Enterprise system

Many vendors offer products in more than one category of software solutions. These software applications are used to merge variable data into static or non-varying elements of a design.

Workstation-based. Workstation-based applications run completely on a computer workstation. The static and variable images are planned and assembled on the workstation. Some of the software applications may work in conjunction with others to produce the final product. Prior to leaving the workstation, however, the design is completed.

Image personalization. Image personalization applications allow personalized or variable information to be incorporated directly into an image. For instance, a person's name could be incorporated into a design by becoming part of the image. An example would be writing someone's name in the sky as if it were written by an actual airplane (figure 3-4). The application would create a graphic image that could then be saved and incorporated into a VDP layout as a variable image. Examples of software capable of image personalization are DirectSmile and the most recent versions of Adobe Photoshop and Adobe Illustrator.

Stand-alone. Stand-alone applications allow for import of either an EPS or PDF file into the application for static elements. The variable information is then added within the stand-alone application. Stand-alone applications include Atlas Printshop Mail, Pageflex Persona, and BCC Mail Manager 2010.

Plug-in. Plug-in applications work in conjunction with an existing program to assist in incorporating and merging the data into the static elements. Plug-in applications work with Adobe InDesign,

Figure 3-4. *An example of image personalization.*

Adobe Acrobat, or QuarkXPress. Applications working directly in InDesign and Quark provide more flexibility in design and more capabilities inherent in the page layout programs. Editing and revising is more easily accomplished if it can be done within the design application.

A plug-in used with Adobe Acrobat is more limited in that the static elements are not easily editable with a PDF file. A plug-in to Acrobat could be more beneficial if the static page is designed by one person, such as a designer, and the variable information is then added by someone else, such as someone in the prepress department of a digital printer. Plug-in applications include Creo Darwin, Printable FusionPro Desktop, and XMPie.

Darwin works with both Quark and InDesign. As seen in figure 3-5, the variable elements can be added to the page design through the use of the Darwin View, Darwin Preview, Darwin Fields and Rules, and Darwin VI Properties.

Dynamic layout. Other types of VDP software have a fixed form and content. Dynamic layout software allows the form and content to be separate. This provides more flexibility when designing for variable content. If a field contains a picture element and there are various size pictures contained in the database, the dynamic

Figure 3-5. *The Darwin View, Darwin Fields and Rules, and Darwin VI Properties dialog boxes.*

layout software will adjust the layout to accommodate for the varying sizes. The dynamic changes can be applied to both graphic and text elements. Examples of dynamic layout software include PageFlex and NimbleFish.

Enterprise system. Enterprise systems are specialized software applications that are primarily code-based and are used exclusively within a particular company or business. This type of software can be very robust and can be largely responsible for digitally managing virtually everything within an organization.

An example of an enterprise system is Oracle. Oracle is known for its database capabilities, but Oracle also provides solutions for a company's email, calendaring, transactions, and more. Some specialized VDP software such as Extream Dialogue is targeted specifically towards the transactional printing industry and is capable of professional design directly within the program. Much of the software used to create transactional documents can be put into the category of enterprise systems. Some enterprise systems do transactional printing and a lot more however.

ROLE OF THE DIGITAL FRONT END

Once a design is completed using a combination of software applications, it is then ready to print to an output device. The next step in the workflow process is the send the file to a ***digital front end (DFE).*** A DFE is a raster image processor (RIP) and more. Not only can DFEs rasterize (rip) files, but they can also impose documents, color-manage files, archive files, and implement variable-data printing. In the past, RIPs were a bottleneck in the workflow for outputting jobs. Today, with the powerful computing options, vendors have developed powerful DFEs that can be scalable to one's particular needs.

Vendors can include as little or as much processing power as needed. Often times a DFE system will contain more than one computer. As more computers are added to the system, the more powerful the system becomes. If a company is processing primarily static jobs or small VDP jobs, less processing power is required. It they are processing large VDP jobs with thousands and thousands of records, more processing power is needed. VDP jobs in which some of the variable information is graphics can also require additional processing power.

With VDP jobs, DFEs play a critical role. Static data is rasterized (ripped) once, and the variable data is then ripped separately. This allows DFEs to be more efficient by not requiring each page to be ripped each time. The static elements are cached at the DFE while the variable elements are ripped for each separate record. The DFE allows the static and variable elements to be ripped separately but printed together. Can you imagine how much processing power would be needed to rasterize a VDP job with 2000 records if it needed to rasterize each page separately? DFEs for VDP have the robust processing power and efficiency needed to create the finished product. DFEs will be discussed in more detail in chapter 4.

WEB-BASED APPLICATIONS

Web-based applications can be used to create VDP jobs by using a website to put together the elements. They are designed to incorporate web pages into the content creation. Two types of web pages can be generated for incorporation into a marketing campaign. A ***static web page*** can be created as a landing page to direct a group of people to, and a ***personalized web page*** can be created as a landing page for a single individual. As Internet use increases for both individual use and business use, web pages will become more and more a media of choice.

A static web page can be used as a marketing tool to an individual to pull information in or as an option for business to design and generate VDP. The advantage of being able to pull information from an individual can contribute greatly to the overall marketing campaign. Once an individual lands on your web page, they have already shown an interest in what you are selling. If you can then get that person to provide you with information such as a name, email address, and mailing address, you can incorporate them into a personalized marketing campaign. You can generate an already designed printed piece, including some personalized information and then mail them that personalized piece. You've now pulled some information from them and then pushed marketing information out to them. They have now become an addition to your marketing database.

Another use for static web pages related to VDP is for members of a company to design and order their own variable-data pieces from a website. The real estate industry lends itself well to this model. Real estate agents can access a website and choose from a variety of templates to design a printed piece. They can upload pictures of a particular listing and also a picture of themselves. They can even upload their customer database for incorporation into the personalized piece. Once it is created, the piece can be printed and either sent to the real estate agent or directly to the customer through a digital printer specializing in offering such a service. Software that allows for web page creation combined with design and production of VDP include Printables' ProFusion, XMPie, and Saepio Technologies.

Another type of web-to-print application is incorporation of a personalized web page with a corresponding personalized URL. The idea behind creating a personalized URL is to use direct mail to link a person to a given website. Let's say you have a mailing list of 5,000 potential customers. A business reply card (BRC) could be created and mailed to the list. The card would include information on what is being marketed, but it would also include at least two options to respond. One would be a toll-free number for someone to call. The other would be a personalized URL such as pennybennett.directoffer.com. If someone sees their name in a URL, they are more likely to respond and go to that web page.

Depending on what is known about the person, the personalized web page can also contain variable information. The web page might contain one type of offer if the person is an existing customer, and a different type of offer if the person is a potential new customer. Response rates and conversions are generally much higher in campaigns that incorporate personalized URLs. A ***conversion*** can be defined as getting someone to take action, whether it be providing more information or making a purchase.

Another benefit of using personalized URLs is the ability to track respondents and update or gather information. It is able to pick up where direct mail leaves off. It can work in conjunction with VDP for a more relevant and personalized marketing campaign. This will be discussed in more detail in chapter 11, "Cross-Media Personalized Marketing." If the personalized URL is being used to gather or update information, it is important to populate that web page with the known information. Users are more likely to respond if it is more convenient for them to do so. Software applications that can generate personalized URLs include XMPie, Mindfire Inc.'s LookWho'sClicking, and Printables' PrintOne Customer Center.

SOFTWARE SELECTION

There are many factors involved in deciding what software or combination of software to use for VDP. Will the software be used to generate personalized print pieces or are personalized URLs a requirement as well? Will there be transactional or other custom uses for the software? How many records will be processed at a time? Who will be doing the database management? Who will be doing the primary layout and design? Where will the variable elements be incorporated?

Much will depend on the level of VDP that is required. Many of the web-to-print options provide a good solution for the printer just starting in VDP. If cross-media campaigns are a necessity then that will require software capable of creating the personalized URL's. Much will also depend on who is involved with the data management and design of the VDP job. If an outside designer is used and then the variable elements are added at the digital printer's location, a stand-alone program might work well allowing all the static information to be imported into the software intact. A plug-in program that uses PDF files as the static elements might work well also in this case. If the printer is doing much of the design and data incorporation, a plug-in application might work better. When it comes to building business rules, it is nice to have a software program that is intuitive to the user so data is accurately merged into the static information.

Some software is specifically designed to print VDP more transactional in nature. Some also have all the proper data cleansing and management tools built into the software. Still others are designed to handle large varieties of variable elements including text and graphics. Some software requires certain hardware configurations to operate efficiently while others will run smoothly on most desktop computes. Software selection should be done carefully to ensure that the right product is chosen for the right use.

4. Workflow

INTRODUCTION

The process of getting a digital file prepared and printed is known as ***workflow.*** The workflow for digital printing is more streamlined than the workflow for traditional printing. There are fewer production steps in digital printing. A traditional printing workflow includes steps needed to make a printing plate. This may include making film from an imagesetter and then making a plate or going directly to plate in a computer-to-plate (CTP) workflow. Digital printing is direct-to-press so the workflow is more efficient. Some of the steps are similar, however.

JOB FLOW

The job flow for digital printing is similar to that of traditional printing. Static digital printing is considerably less complicated than VDP. The job flow for VDP will differ some in that it has a database and VDP software as part of the overall flow. The basic job flow that exists for all types of digital printing incorporates some type of design, certain graphic elements, and some type of output. The software and file formats that can be used in the job flow can vary greatly. Figure 4-1 shows the job flow for static digital printing prior to sending the project to the printer.

A page design is created that would most likely include a page layout, some graphics, and some fonts. Someone needs to create the initial design. This is sometimes called the ***content creator.*** The content creator can be the client or person desiring the finished product, a graphic designer, a prepress provider, an ad agency, or some type of marketing personnel. Generally speaking, static digital printing will draw a wider variety of content creators from many walks of life depending on the complexity of the printed piece.

Desktop publishing has put the tools in the hands of many for content creation. If someone has a computer and a desktop printer, they are certainly capable of content creation for output on a digital press. Outputting to a digital press can sometimes be as simple as FILE>PRINT. Large organizations may have digital

Figure 4-1. Job flow for static digital printing prior to sending the project to the printer.

presses networked so many people within the organization can print directly to the digital press. The lines are becoming blurred between a digital printer, digital copier, and digital press. Some organizations will have all of these available on the network for various personnel to print to directly.

The level of knowledge a content creator has for good file preparation may affect the ability to output correctly, however. As there is more of a shift to PDF creation directly from layout and design applications, it is likely the trend will continue with having a wide variety of people doing content creation.

Content creation for VDP is more challenging and will likely not involve as wide a range of people because of the complexity and increased number of steps in the overall job flow. Figure 4-2 shows the job flow for VDP prior to sending the job to the printer. Page design is still part of the job flow, but working with data, defining rules for applying the data and merging the data, are also part of the job flow for VDP.

The complexity increases due to the incorporation of databases and the need for some type of VDP software that allows for incorporation of both the static and variable elements. A layout

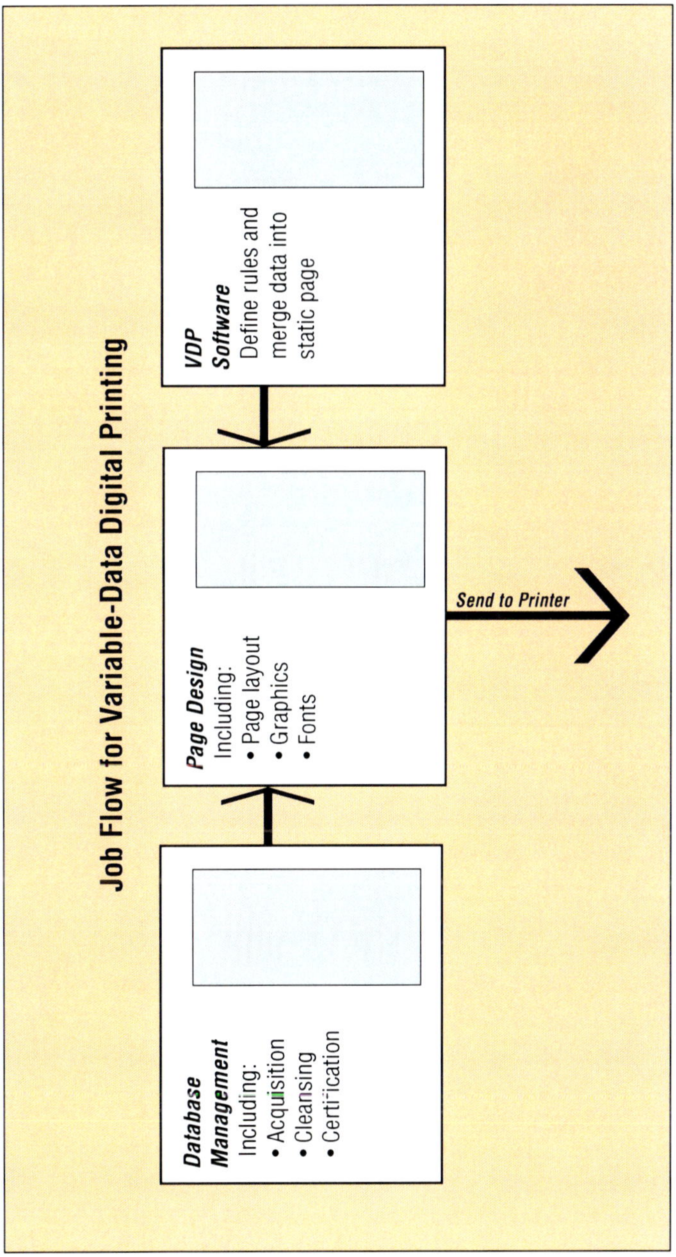

Figure 4-2. *Job flow for variable-data digital printing prior to sending the project to the printer.*

and design application is needed at some point in the job flow. The variable information can be included in the process, depending on what type of software is used.

There is likely to be more than one person involved in the job flow for VDP. Working with databases isn't typically a skill that a content creator would have. VDP content creation is less likely to have the wide variety of skill levels involved in putting a VDP piece together. Content creators working with VDP designs will need a very sophisticated level of understanding and experience for the job to be successful. Outputting a VDP job is not as simple as outputting a static digital printing job. The output format needs to be compatible with the digital front end (DFE). Since each piece is unique, it is critical that every piece print in a VDP job. It may also be necessary to print extra "dummy" pieces if some type of makeready is needed for setup of finishing operations such as folding, addressing, or inserting.

NETWORKING

When people network with one another they develop connections from people they know to people they don't know. As human beings we network with one another in both our professional and personal lives. Usually there is a purpose for someone wanting to network with other people. There are similarities to computer networking. Computer networking is developing connections between various components of the computer system. Typically this would include workstations, servers, digital front ends, and marking engines. These devices are connected by either hard wire connections, wireless connections, or both.

The methods used for implementing a connection between devices is an important consideration primarily because of transfer speed and security. The most popular and most reliable method of connecting computers together is using ***Ethernet*** as the cabling system and ***Transfer Control Protocol/Internet Protocol (TCP/IP)*** as the transfer protocol. Ethernet provides the ability to transfer large files very quickly over a network. TCP/IP is a very good protocol for managing computers in a secure environment.

A ***workstation*** is a computer that is used for work production and is connected to a network. A workstation can be either a Macintosh or a PC. Almost all workstations today have Ethernet ports and the option for wireless connectivity as well. Implementing a wireless network is less work and requires less time investment in building the infrastructure. Hard-wired connections, such as Ethernet, are generally better for speed and reliability.

The workstation will be connected to the DFE via the network. Most DFEs have Ethernet connections as the input method, but a different configuration is generally used for outputting from the DFE to the marking engine. Most digital presses use a proprietary cabling system for connection between the DFE and the marking engine. It may even be a series of cables. Often times, because the ripped data is very large, special cabling is needed to move the data quickly to the marking engine. The DFE can also be used for storing and archiving files or a separate server can be set up for file storage and archiving. If a separate server is used, it must also be part of the overall network. Figure 4-3 shows a typical network in a digital press environment.

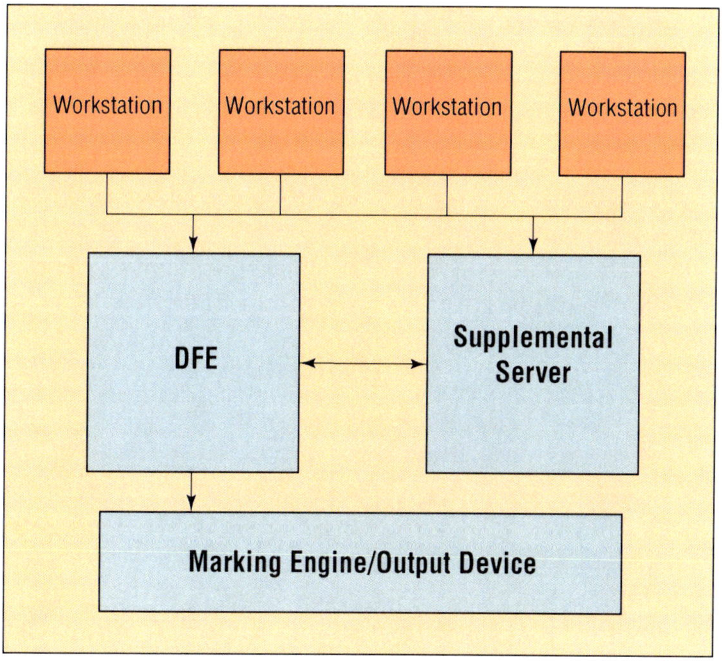

Figure 4-3. *A typical network in a digital press environment.*

OPERATOR-CONTROLLED DIGITAL PRINTING

Most digital presses also have the added option of an operator-controlled unit. This is usually a connected or separate unit that allows for scanning and digital conversion of analog data into digital format for output to the digital press. The Xerox DigiPath (now part of FreeFlow) is an example of this. The operator-controlled unit provides a convenience for non-digital reproduction. Caution must be used regarding loss of quality using the scanning input, however. Any time an original is scanned there will be some loss in quality on the reproduction from the original. If a digital file is available for output, this method is preferred to the scanning input method. Sometimes that is not an option though.

Some operator-controlled units have the ability to store and archive scanned data as well. The units also will have the ability to control the digital press in almost every aspect that is available as part of the DFE including paper size, paper color, duplexing, collation, and binding options.

DIGITAL FRONT END

A ***digital front end (DFE)*** is a system that connects and outputs to the print engine or the digital press itself. So how does a DFE differ from a raster image processor (RIP)? A DFE contains a RIP but today can do much more than just ripping. DFEs can also create documents, impose jobs, control color, job management via the Internet or intranet, archive jobs, automate workflow, proof, access databases, and balance print load between printers based on a distribute-and-print model. Distribute-and-print allows for one file to print at many locations. Under this model, the DFE doesn't necessarily need to be connected directly to the print engine.

Gordon Moore, a Silicon Valley pioneer, developed something called ***Moore's Law,*** which states that computing power doubles every 18 months. Even without testing his law, it is easy to see that the computing power has increased dramatically and this has benefited the print world tremendously. In the past, the print engine could print faster than the RIP could process the files. This is not the case any more. Today's DFEs not only have fast processors but also multiprocessors in most cases. In fact, a DFE system can also be multiple computers. Since the processing power was once a bottleneck, this would place limits on what could be processed in terms of color, number of records, or image files used within a particular VDP job. These limits no longer exist so the level of sophistication and what can be accomplished for VDP production is almost limitless.

In the past, customers were limited with their choices for DFEs because proprietary systems would be the only option for driving a particular print engine. Today, many companies make DFEs for a variety of print engines. Manufacturers of DFEs and print engines are working closely together to help provide more options and more robust features than ever before. Manufacturers will configure a DFE depending on the needs of the customer. They market it as a comprehensive solution designed to meet the customer's needs. The features are usually sold in modules and are sometimes actually a separate software application installed on the DFE. For example, the EFI Fiery DFE has the ability to impose documents. It is done with a software application called DocBuilder Pro. Once a file is sent to the DFE and it appears in the print queue, the option is available to impose the document. Once that option is selected, DocBuilder Pro opens to configure the document further. A separate, imposed file is then created and placed back into the print queue.

CONTROLLING SYSTEM

Along with the DFE, a digital press will also have a controlling system connected directly to the digital press itself. This controlling unit has the ability to specify different paper types within certain trays, if sheetfed. It can also monitor and manage the consumables such as paper and toner/ink. If a paper tray runs out or if a toner cartridge runs too low, the controlling system will notify the operator of the status.

MARKING ENGINE

The ***marking engine*** is the actual digital press itself. This is sometimes called a ***print engine*** but a broader term is marking engine. Not all output devices will ultimately print. For example, an imagesetter or platesetter places a mark on film or a plate but doesn't necessarily print. In digital printing, marking engine and print engine can be used interchangeably.

Once the digital file is rasterized by the RIP, it is then sent to the marking engine. The raster dots will either be imaged or not. The marking engine has a maximum ***resolution*** of dots per inch (dpi) that it is capable of reproducing. A digital press with a 2400-dpi output resolution is going to reproduce a finer dot than a digital press with a 600-dpi output resolution.

As the raster file is sent to the marking engine, each raster dot will either be on or off. If it is on, the marking engine will make an image in that area. If the raster dot is off, it will not make an image in that area. Marking engines can image dots based on the particular technology of the digital press. It may be a dot of dry toner or liquid toner, or it may be an inkjet dot.

Although the marking engine's primary task is to create an image on a substrate, there are sometimes in-line auxiliary operations that can be performed before the product is finished. A webfed digital press can have the ability to cut the roll into sheets as the paper comes off the press. Or a sheetfed press could have the ability to collate, staple, or perform some other type of in-line finishing.

5. Digital Print Production

DESIGNING FOR DIGITAL PRINT

Introduction. Designing for digital printing has many similarities to designing for traditional printing and many of the same basic principles apply, but some things are also different. Digital printing has some advantages and disadvantages compared to traditional printing. One basic principle that still applies though is to always check with the printer when questions arise. Communication between the designer or content creator and digital printer is still an essential component for success. Each digital press may have slightly different limitations and requirements, and the printer is still the best one to know what those are and how to prepare accordingly.

There are things that need to be considered in print production when designing as well. Is it black-and-white or color, or how about a blend of both? Are they all process colors? Are there any spot colors? What resolution and color mode should the graphics be? Is there a color management system in place? In what format should the file(s) be submitted? What type of paper will be used? How will that affect the job? Are there any finishing processes to be done?

File preparation. Good file preparation is important to the success of a digitally printed job. This includes knowing and understanding things like graphic file formats, resolution, color modes, file management, understanding fonts, trapping and imposition, preflighting, and file transportation. Digital printing is a form of custom production—meaning every job can be quite different. It is very important for the content creator and printer to communicate during all stages of production. There should be no such thing as a stupid question regarding good file preparation. It is in the best interest of everyone involved to make sure custom jobs print correctly. This can only be done through good communication about all of the issues previously mentioned.

Designing backwards. Designing for digital printing, as well as traditional printing, requires designing from the back end to the front end. What this means is that you must understand what takes place in the bindery and in print production to maximize the best design for output on digital presses. A simple example in bindery would be something like a three-fold brochure. Most people would think that you just divide a page in thirds and start placing your images on the page. If this is done, the final printed image will not match the fold properly. Let's take a closer look. You're designing a brochure that has a finished trim size of $8\frac{1}{2}\times11$ in. (215.9×279.4 mm). The page will be designed in a landscape format. If you divide the 11-in. width by three, you have three panels that are approximately $3\frac{2}{3}$ in. (93.2 mm) each. But this won't work when it is folded. Instead, one panel—the panel that is on the inside when folded—needs to be slightly smaller than the other two panels. Therefore, two panels should be $3\frac{11}{16}$ in. (93.7 mm) and one panel should be $3\frac{5}{8}$ in. (92.1 mm), as shown in figure 5-1. If it is a two-sided brochure, then each side will need to be composed a little differently. When designing the inside and outside of the brochure, the smallest panel of $3\frac{5}{8}$ in. will change sides on the design.

Bleeds. When designing a job, it is also important to know how to set bleeds and how much of a bleed to set. Standard bleed amounts are $\frac{1}{16}$ in. (1.6 mm) to $\frac{1}{8}$ in. (3.2 mm), but it is always best to check with the printer. It is also important to communicate with the printer that you have set bleeds within the design. Knowing the final trim size and any binding requirements are essential as well. Digital presses, just like traditional presses, are not capable of printing right up to the edge of the sheet. So in order to achieve a bleed, the design must be printed on paper larger than the finished piece and then trimmed back. Digital printing may be limited by the maximum sheet size. If 12×18 in. (304.8×457.2 mm) is the maximum sheet size of a given digital press, the maximum finished size with a full bleed is likely to be 11×17 in. (279.4×431.8 mm).

Graphic file formats. Graphics used for digital printing are much different than graphics used for digital display such as a website or multimedia. Graphics used for digital printing must contain more information than graphics that will ultimately be

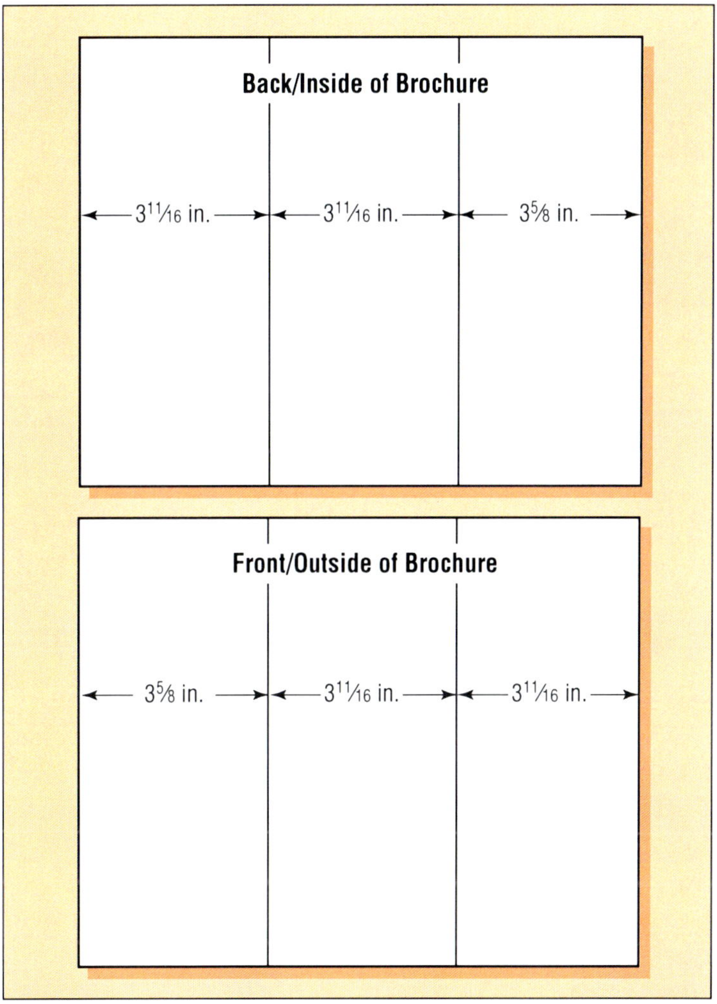

Figure 5-1. *Correct dimensions of tri-fold brochure to ensure proper folding.*

displayed on a projector or monitor. Graphic files are usually some type of illustration or a photograph. Illustrations are usually created using an illustration program such as Adobe Illustrator. Scanning an original photograph or using a digital camera usually creates a digital photograph. Digital photographs are usually captured or edited in Adobe Photoshop. Most graphics are created

Figure 5-2. *A raster graphic is made up of pixels. (Reprinted from* Color and Its Reproduction, Third Edition)

either using pixels to create an image (as shown in figure 5-2), or a series of points and paths to create and image (as shown in figure 5-3). Graphics made up of pixels are called ***raster graphics,*** while graphics made with points and paths are called ***vector graphics.***

Graphic files can be kept in their native file format such as Illustrator (.ai) files or Photoshop (.psd) files, but it is generally better to save the file as either a ***tagged image file format (TIFF)*** file or ***encapsulated PostScript (EPS)*** file and then place that file into the page-layout program. TIFF is the most common raster graphic file format used for digital printing. EPS is the most common vector graphic file format used for digital printing. Other graphic file formats can be used but caution must be used regarding

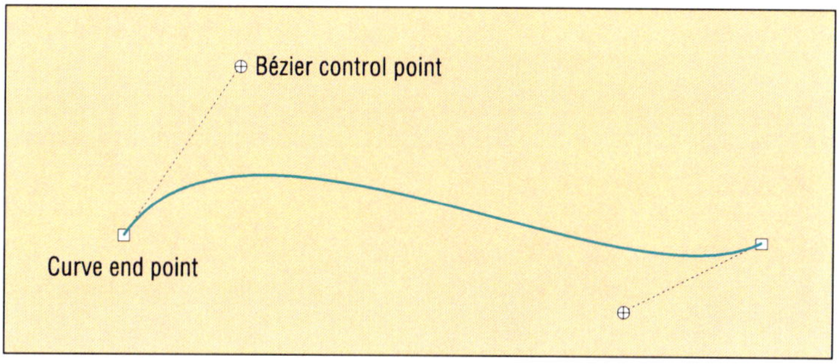

Figure 5-3. Vector graphics consist of mathematically described points, lines, and arcs. Shown here is a bézier curve, one of the building blocks of vector graphics. The shape of the curve is controlled by the two "handles," or control points.

compatibility and quality. Today, most digital images are captured by digital cameras which, by default, save files as JPEG (Joint Photographic Experts Group). JPEG is a good graphic file format for digital camera use because of the compression capabilities inherent in the format. Caution must be used with JPEG, however, because it is based on ***lossy compression*** which means quality is lost and vital pixel information may be thrown away. The best thing to do with a digital image captured from a digital camera is to open it in Photoshop, resize to the desired size, and resave in a TIFF format for export into the page-layout program. JPEG is commonly used for preparing graphics for websites as is ***graphics interchange format (GIF),*** but neither are recommended for reproduction on digital presses.

Image resolution and resizing. Image resolution is measured and defined by the amount of pixels that are contained in the original file. Images are captured on digital cameras in terms of megapixels, and images are scanned on scanners by capturing a defined amount of ***pixels per inch (ppi).*** This is sometimes referred to as ***input resolution. Output resolution*** is the capabilities of a given output device and is measured in terms of ***dots per inch (dpi).*** A digital press may have the capability to output at 600 dpi or 2400 dpi. People sometimes use the terms "dpi" and "ppi" synonymously, but in fact they are quite different. Both are types of resolution, but "ppi" refers to input resolution and is representing pixels, while "dpi" refers to output resolution and is referring to the dots turned on or off by the RIP once the file goes to the marking engine. A dot of toner or a dot of ink is either imaged or it is not. It is important to make a distinction between these two for better communication in the industry. If a designer or content creator asks a printer to "increase the resolution," is the person referring to "ppi" or "dpi"? One more type of output resolution is ***lines per inch,*** or ***lpi.*** This is also sometimes called ***screen frequency*** and is referring to the rows of lines or dots in a printed halftone. This can be determined by the substrate being used and/or the capabilities of the digital press. It is always best to check with your printer to determine the most appropriate screen frequency for a given job or a given digital press.

A general rule, then, is to capture the input resolution (ppi) at twice the known screen frequency (lpi). If the printer determines that the press is capable of reproducing 150-lpi halftones, then the input resolution should be 300 ppi. A good minimum input resolution in today's world of print reproduction is 300 ppi. Even if it is determined that the digital press can reproduce only the equivalent of a 100-lpi halftone, the small amount of oversampling in this case isn't likely going to hinder production. Line art should be treated a little differently and should be captured at a resolution of 1200 ppi.

The final size of a graphic is also very important. Most digital cameras today will capture more than enough digital information for reproduction on a digital press. It is important to be sure that the graphic does not contain too much information as it will slow down the network and the RIP, but too little information will result in low-quality graphic reproduction. For example, a typical five-megapixel camera will capture an image at 300 ppi that is approximately 6½×8½ in. (165.1×215.9 mm). The file size will be just over 14 megabytes (MB). But if that file is only going to reproduce at 5×7 in. (127.0×177.8 mm), the image size can be reduced and Photoshop can resample the image—making the file size around 9 MB (figure 5-4). This may not seem like a lot of savings in file size, but multiple pictures and multiple pages can increase transfer time and output time significantly. It is important to resize a file in Photoshop and not within the page-layout program as Photoshop actually reduces the file size whereas page-layout

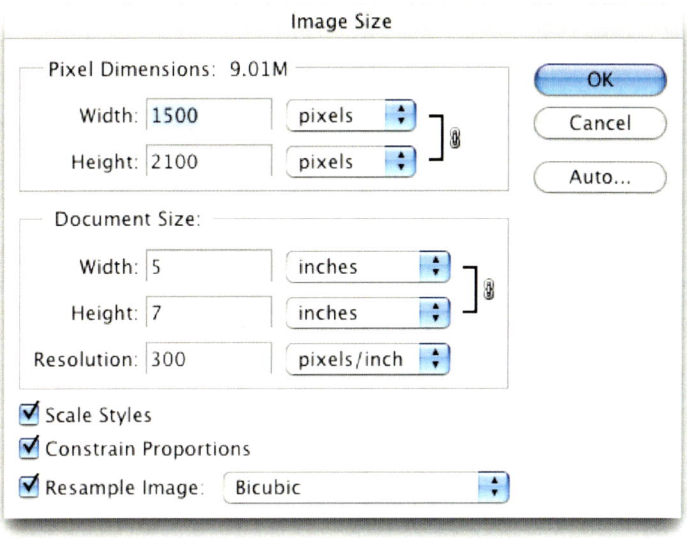

Figure 5-4. Image size—and file size—can be reduced by resampling the image in Adobe Photoshop, as shown in the above dialog box.

programs only reduce the view with the program but does not reduce the file size.

Resizing a raster graphic to a larger scale is generally not a good idea. This only increases the pixel size and therefore reduces the overall quality of the graphic. Photoshop can actually increase the resolution of a graphic but is does this by interpolating, or guessing, what pixel information to add. The end result is a higher-resolution graphic, but a lower-quality reproduction.

As previously mentioned, graphics from websites are not designed for use in digital printing. Most web graphics are at a fixed resolution of 72 ppi so they will load quickly when viewing websites. Small file sizes are important for web graphics but not for graphics destined for digital printing. Don't confuse this with purchasing high-resolution graphics over the Internet, however. Many companies provide high-resolution graphics over the Internet, but there is usually a fee associated with them. If you are designing a digital printing job for a company that also has a website, be sure to get high-resolution graphics from the company rather than taking the company's logo or graphics off the website.

Color mode. Graphic images are usually captured by digital camera or scanner in additive colors of red, green, and blue ***(RGB).*** The final product is usually printed in some type of process color environment of cyan, magenta, yellow, and black ***(CMYK).*** RGB has a larger color space than CMYK. In the traditional printing environment, it is customary to change RGB files into CMYK files prior to outputting. In the digital printing environment that is not necessarily the case. Many digital presses today have CMYK with other inks or toners added to the mix, such as a light cyan and light magenta. There may be other proprietary process color systems instead of CMYK. Since the RGB color space is pretty large, it is best to investigate the output before making a conversion. If a simple conversion to CMYK is done in Photoshop, critical color information could be lost in the process. Many DFEs have algorithms built specifically for a particular digital press to make a conversion from RGB to CMYK or other specified color models depending on the press configurations. So the conversions and separations may be done within the RIP. If this is the case, the graphic files should remain in RGB format until output. It is best to check with the printer to determine what color mode would best suit the workflow before converting.

Some digital presses even have the ability to reproduce custom or ***spot colors.*** The spot colors are either converted at the RIP to a close approximation or some presses even have the ability to add specialty spot colors as a separate printing toner or ink. As the trend for brighter, more vibrant colors continues, and short-run color shifts more to the consumer packaging segment, the demand for digital presses to reproduce larger color gamuts or custom color printing will continue.

SPECIAL DESIGN CONSIDERATIONS

Some digital presses have certain reproduction limitations or sometimes they just reproduce differently than a traditional printing so some considerations must be made related to design. For example type can sometimes reproduce differently as can printing in solid areas or reproducing grays.

Blacks. Most digital presses today have the capability to produce a very dark black for solid black areas, in some cases more so than printing black in a traditional printing environment. Sometimes the blacks can be enhanced, however, by adding more color to the black. This is referred to as a ***rich black*** or ***super black***. Super blacks are nothing more than black with other colors added to it. For example, the designer could specify a color of 100% black, plus 50% cyan, 40% magenta, and 40% yellow (figure 5-5). This would likely create a deeper, richer black (hence the term "rich black") on the finished product. Another option would be to print 100% black, plus 60 or 80% of one of the other process colors. The results would be a deep black with a slight hue of the process color added to the mix. This can provide a creative option for designers looking to differentiate the look of a design.

Figure 5-5. *The block at the left is printed in black only. The block at the right is a rich black or super black, printed with 100% black, 50% cyan, 40% magenta, and 40% yellow.*

In traditional printing, most presses have a limit of ***total ink coverage***. For example, it is not advisable to print 100% of each process color as adverse effects happen due to the large amounts of ink accumulating in one area. In this case, more is not necessarily better. This is also true of digital printing. Most digital presses have a total "ink" limit as well even if it is toner being laid down rather than ink. It is best to check with the press manufacturer or printer prior to specifying large percentages for super blacks. You can expect that total number to be somewhere in the range of 250% to 300% total coverage. What this means is that a super black of 100% black, 60% cyan, 60% magenta, and 60% yellow—representing a total coverage of 280%—may be dangerously close to exceeding the press's total coverage limits.

Solids. One thing that digital presses don't always do well is print large areas of solid colors evenly. Often times what happens is the area has some type of ***banding*** or blending problems. The result is a poor-looking solid area. One option is to avoid designing large areas of solid color, but this isn't really practical. If gray is the color to be reproduced, it is best to use tints of black rather than a process mix and it may also be best to specify tints of 20% or higher and 80% or lower. Another option is to create some type of noise in the design to help improve the blending. This can be done by adding some type of pattern to a solid area or using Photoshop's noise filters to create a subtle pattern. Another option would be to reduce the amount of overall color as lighter areas seem to reproduce better than darker areas.

Type. Very small type should be avoided in designs destined for digital printing for a couple of reasons. The average readable type is set at 10 to 12 points (pt.). Some digital presses can reproduce type smaller than that, but it should be assessed as to the overall readability of type smaller than ten points. Although some digital presses can print type as small as 4 pt., the readability of 4-pt. type may be a broader question to ask.

Reverse type can also be reproduced nicely on most digital presses, but if you want to ensure better results, consider making a super black as described earlier but try using less black, especially for small type or fonts with fine letter forms and serifs. It is also best when reproducing reverse type to use a bright white stock to help the type stand out better.

The color of the type or the background color can have an effect on the final printed piece from a digital press as well. If the type is going to be printed in any color other than black, some consideration should be given to the outcome. Type that is too light is difficult to read. If a legible color is used for the type, it is best to use at least 80% of any of the process colors (cyan, magenta, and black) except yellow. Yellow is too light and won't give the desired effect like the other colors. Similarly, if white type is going to be on a colored background the same rule applies. If there is at least 80% of one of the process colors (cyan, magenta, and black except yellow) in the background, the type will knock out better.

One other thing to consider related to reproducing type on digital presses is the need to overprint black text on a colored background, especially if it is a light background. Sometimes digital presses will create a slight halo around type because the default is to knock out the text. Once the type is set to overprint, it should significantly reduce or eliminate the halo effect.

Good type reproduction is highly dependent on use of fonts and good font selection. Fonts will be discussed later in greater detail, but it is important to mention the use of type styles when designing with type. Most applications have a type style button or menu that allows for applying styles such as bold and italic. It is important, however, not to apply styles in this way. It is better to use the actual digital font to apply the style. For example, the font Bookman can be chosen and then have the software apply an italic style to it. But it is always preferred to actually choose the font Bookman Italic from the font menu. This will provide consistent results and doesn't require the software to simulate the desired effect.

Paper and proofing. In the early development of digital presses, paper stocks were limited. This is not the case today. Virtually any type of stock desired can be acquired and printed on many digital presses. However, it is always best to consult with the printer regarding paper choices. Since digital presses require virtually no makeready, it is easier to request testing or proofing at various stages of production. If there is any doubt about the reproducibility of any of the issues discussed already, it is perfectly reasonable to have a proof made during the process to determine the outcome.

Proofs can be done early on as a concept proof or also as a final or contract proof prior to full production. Proofing and reproduction of spot colors has always been a challenge in traditional printing environments. Prior to digital proofing, spot colors could be proofed using analog laminate proofing systems such as MatchPrint. Today, digital proofing may or may not be able to accurately represent what color the spot color will actually print on a traditional printing press. With digital presses this is not an issue, however, because the actual production press can be used to generate the contract proof. It removes any of the guesswork or variability out of communicating how a particular color will reproduce. If there is a question as to how a particular super black will reproduce, it is easy to test it on the digital press.

FONTS

Whenever a particular font is chosen to use in a document, the font information that allows it to look the way it does on the screen and when printed comes from a digital font file(s) stored locally on the machine on which the document was created. When the document file is transported to another machine, such as to a printing company, the digital font file(s) must be transported as well. Content creators aren't always aware of this. Therefore, the most common problem associated with successful output of files is missing fonts. On a Macintosh platform fonts are dealt with differently depending on whether that Mac is operating under OS 9 or OS X (pronounced OS ten).

In OS 9, fonts are stored either in the Fonts folder within the System folder on the Macintosh or within a font management utility such as Suitcase, ATM Deluxe, or FontReserve. On the Mac, if a large number of fonts are used, a font management utility is a necessity. Currently, the most common type of font used by content creators is PostScript ***Type 1 fonts.*** They are well-known for their quality and reliable output. Most printers prefer PostScript Type 1 fonts. Type 1 fonts, as they are sometimes called, have both a screen font and printer font (figure 5-6). Screen fonts are normally stored in a suitcase. A suitcase is just a special kind of folder that stores fonts. Font suitcases usually contain either PostScript Type 1 screen fonts or a family of TrueType fonts. Another common font type is ***TrueType fonts.*** TrueType fonts have just one icon rather than the two that are needed by Type 1 fonts. TrueType fonts can also be used but avoid using ***Multiple Master fonts*** and use fonts off the Internet with caution. If they are free fonts, remember, you usually do get what you pay for. Some fonts from unreliable sources can cause output problems on

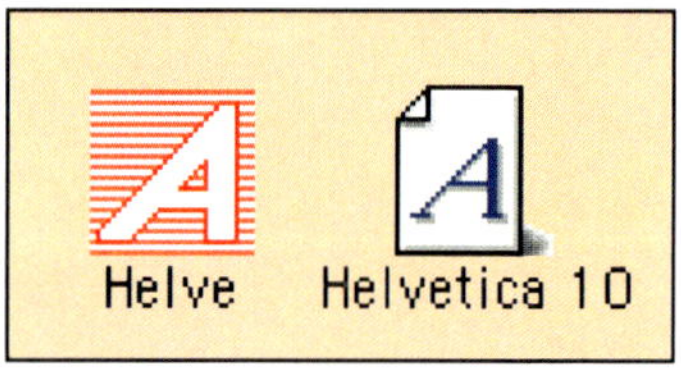

Figure 5-6. *Icons for the printer font (left) and screen font (right) for a Type 1 font.*

digital presses. Another option that will be discussed later is to save files with fonts embedded as PDF.

In OS X, fonts are usually stored in the Fonts folder that is located in the Library. As OS X becomes more fully integrated into production environments, ***Open Type fonts*** will likely become the new standard. Open Type fonts offer over 65,000 characters compared to the 256-character limits in Type 1 and TrueType fonts. Open Type is also a smaller file size and cross-platform compatible making it the ideal source for future font integration. The changeover process will not occur overnight however. Companies won't be eager to invest more money into new fonts as long as their current fonts are meeting their needs.

If a native file is sent to the printer, both QuarkXPress and InDesign offer very nice features for collecting fonts and graphics as well. Quark uses the "Collect for Output" option that allows for collection of both fonts and graphics. By default, Quark does not collect fonts however. It is an option that must be selected in the Collect for Output dialog box, as shown in figure 5-7. It is also important to select both screen fonts and printer fonts. InDesign's font and graphic collection feature is called "Package." By default, it does collect both fonts and graphics without needing to make the selection, as shown in figure 5-8.

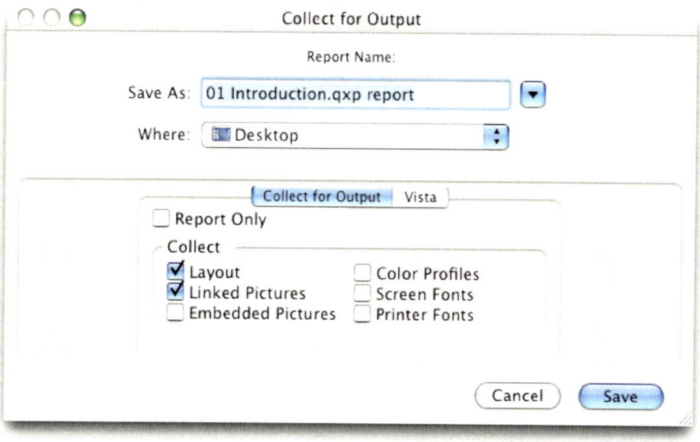

Figure 5-7. *The "Collect for Output" dialog box in QuarkXPress. The defaults are set up to collect linked graphics, but not fonts.*

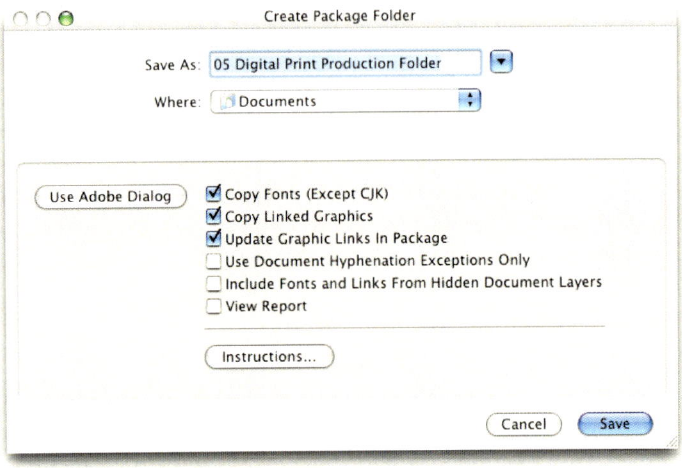

Figure 5-8. The "Create Package Folder" dialog in Adobe InDesign, which is set up to collect fonts and graphics as its default.

If the native file that is sent to the printer is an Adobe Illustrator (.ai) file or an EPS file saved from Illustrator, it might be wise to turn the fonts into graphics using Illustrator's "Create Outlines" feature. Because Illustrator wasn't intended as a page-layout tool, there shouldn't be large amounts of text in a design created in Illustrator. This provides an option to select the text that is in the design and create outlines, thereby turning the actual font into a series of points and paths. The need to include the font with the native file is then eliminated because it is now a PostScript outline.

FILE MANAGEMENT

The digital world has made things so much easier in many ways. Digital data is easily created, easily edited, and easily transferable. It can also be very vulnerable and difficult to manage as well. It is important to have a good system of saving, archiving, and retrieving files. Just as you'd organize your file cabinet with hanging files and folders, your digital files need to be organized with some logical system as well. Depending on the number of files that need to be managed, this can be done manually or with some type of ***digital asset management (DAM)*** system. The important thing is to have some type of system and to have a system for backing up and archiving files.

Digital data can be vulnerable to corruption or loss. Once the data is gone, restoring or retrieving data can be very difficult if not impossible. If there is not a recent backup of the data, this can be disastrous. Today, there are a variety of options for file management including servers, external hard drives, and removable media. It is always a good idea to have an on-site data storage option and an off-site option as well in the event of loss due to fire or other unforeseen circumstances.

It is also important to keep track of the most recent version of a document. This can be checked by the date modified of a given file. Once a graphic file is placed into a illustration or page-layout program, it is important to remember that the graphic is not embedded in the page-layout program, but linked. What this means is that the graphic must stay with the page-layout document. Also, if the graphic is renamed, it should be updated or reimported into the page-layout program.

TRAPPING

Trapping compensates for misregister with adjoining colors in the printing process. (This type of trapping should not be confused with the term ***ink trapping*** that is used to determine how efficiently one ink film lays down on the preceding ink film when printing multiple colors.) When a job is designed that has two or more colors, it may require trapping prior to being printed. When two colors are printed adjacent to each other they should butt right up against each other. Sometimes there will be slight shifting between colors. This can result in an unwanted white line on one side of the object (figure 5-9). To compensate for any movement that may occur between the colors, a technique called trapping is used that creates a slight overlap between the colors. Once a trap is created, any movement will be filled in by the overlap.

With digital presses, the registration is very good, but sometimes trapping is still needed. It is important to know if and where trapping will occur. Sometimes it is done automatically in the DFE. If this is the case, the file should not be trapped prior to being sent to the printer. An exception might be overprinting black text on a light background to prevent a halo effect.

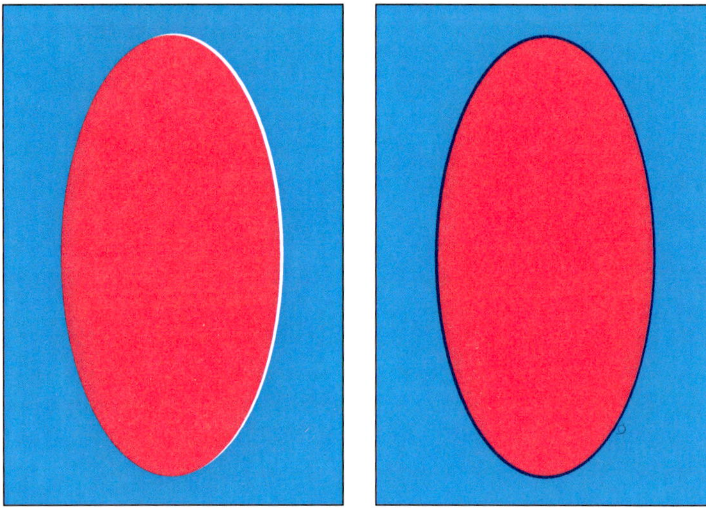

Figure 5-9. Trapping is used to compensate for any misregister that might occur on a printing press. Notice the unwanted white line in the untrapped image at the left.

PREFLIGHTING

Preflighting is the process of checking a file before sending it to a printer or before sending it to an output device. The term comes from the process of preflighting an aircraft before takeoff to ensure the plane won't malfunction and crash. Preflighting in digital file preparation can also prevent the file from crashing the RIP. The process of preflighting can be as simple as manually checking a file to be sure it is set up properly or as sophisticated as using specialized preflighting software to check for certain criteria.

Some of the common problems with files that can be detected by preflighting are missing fonts, missing graphics, low-resolution graphics, graphics in the wrong color mode, and JPEG or GIF graphics. Another thing that should be checked at this stage is the overall layout. Is the job set up to bleed? Are the bleeds set up properly? Is the job supposed to fold? Will the design fit the fold?

Preflighting can be done by the designer/content creator or by the printing professional. Software packages are available for both. Preflighting can also be done through a web interface if the printer has that option available. If files are sent to the printer over the

Internet, an added convenience would be the option to preflight the file prior to sending it off. Adobe InDesign also offers a simple preflighting option, as shown in figure 5-10. It is always best to check with the printer to see what they recommend for preflighting.

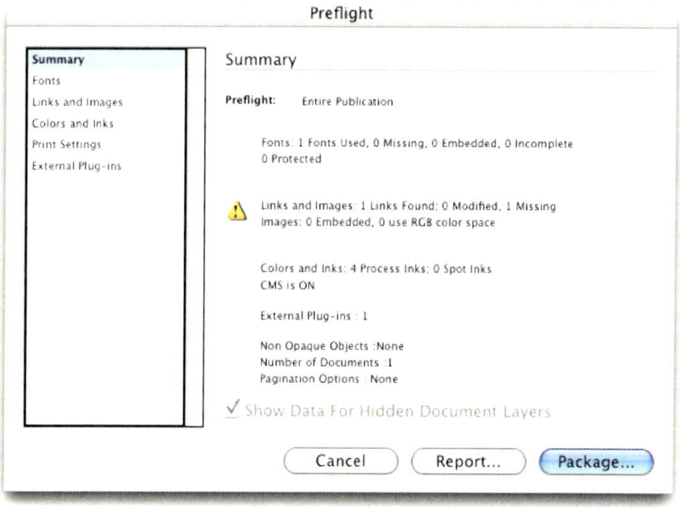

Figure 5-10. *The "Preflight" summary dialog box in Adobe InDesign, indicating that one of the images is missing.*

FILE TRANSPORT

Once a job is ready to send to the printer, there are several ways this can be done. First determine if the printer would like the job sent in its native format or as a PDF file with fonts and graphics embedded. Once that is determined, it should be determined whether the file(s) need to be compressed or not. File compression can increase the transfer time on both the sending and receiving end. If compression is used, it is important to use compression software that uses lossless compression. This means that it will compress files but will not throw out any digital information. When the file(s) are decompressed there should be no lose in quality. Files can be sent either as email attachments, using an FTP server or a WebDAV server. It is best to check with the print provider to determine the best way to send the file.

IMPOSITION, FOLDING, AND FINISHING

Imposition is the process of assembling pages in the proper orientation so when folded and cut, the pages come out in sequential order. Larger printing presses take larger sheet sizes, therefore it is common with large press formats to print multiple pages on one press sheet. This is referred to as a ***signature.*** Signatures are printed on both sides, sometimes referred to as Side A and Side B. Figure 5-11 shows a 32-page signature with 16 pages printed on each side.

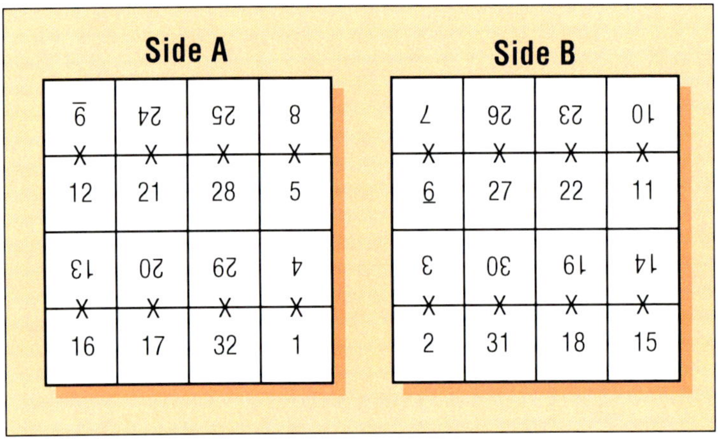

Figure 5-11. *A 32-page imposition, with 16 pages printed on each side. The "X's" indicate the head (or top) of each page.*

Digital presses don't have as large of a sheet size capacity as many large printing presses, but imposition is still needed when multiple pages are printed on a sheet. It is important to understand the difference between a reader's spread and a printer's spread. A ***reader's spread*** would be how two pages are next to each other in the finished book. In other words, how is the reader viewing it? Pages 20 and 21 of a book or magazine, for example, would be a reader's spread, because the pages are across the fold from each other, as shown in figure 5-12. A ***printer's spread*** would be how two pages are viewed on the printed sheet prior to folding and binding. For example, in the 32-page imposition shown in figure 5-11, pages 9 and 24 on side A would be considered a printer's spread.

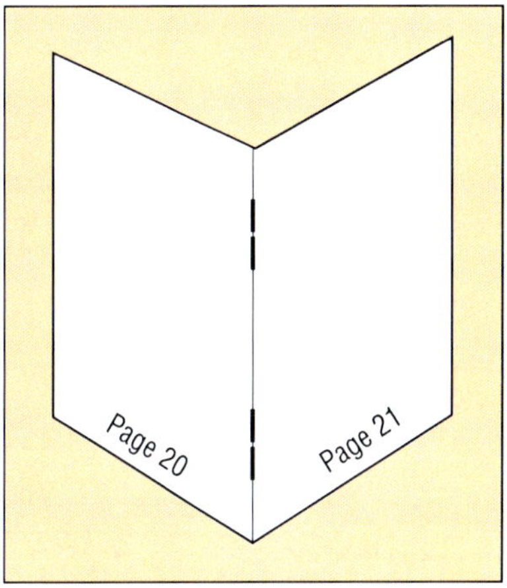

Figure 5-12. *A reader's spread in a magazine.*

Documents can be set up with either reader's spreads or printer's spreads. The important thing is to communicate between the content creator and the printer how it is set up. A ***folding dummy*** or a mock-up should also be provided to the printer for better clarification. Most digital presses have some type of imposition software built into the DFE for handling the particular imposition that works best on a given press. It is important to plan for the proper amount of gutter between pages for the particular binding process that will be used. For example, saddle stitching may require a varying gutter as page counts increase, whereas some type of signature stacking as is common with perfect binding may not require a varying gutter but may require a larger inside gutter for the trimming that occurs in the binding process.

Consideration must also be given to the area that is to be folded. Electrophotography can be susceptible to cracking in folding areas that have heavy coverage. One solution is to design areas to be folded with less coverage. Another option is to plan on ***scoring*** a sheet prior to folding. Scoring will always give the best results for folds, especially with heavier paper stock. Another thing that should be considered for folding is the ***grain direction*** of the paper. When paper is manufactured, the paper fibers tend to align in one direction. If possible, it is always best to plan a fold in the direction of the paper grain. Folding against the grain will likely cause ***cracking*** to occur and usually results in an uneven fold, as shown in figure 5-13.

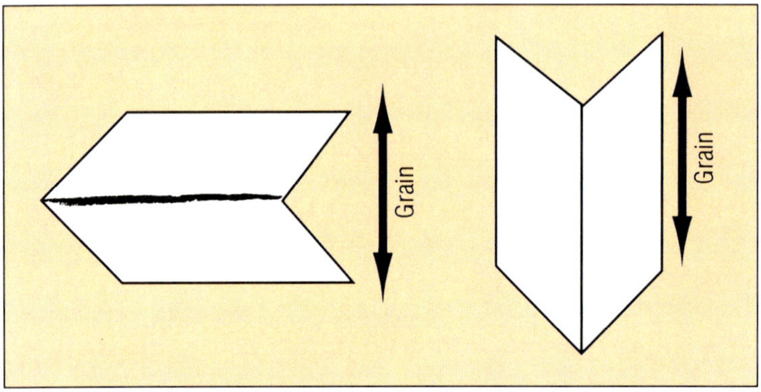

Figure 5-13. Folding against the grain can produce an uneven fold (left) while folding with the grain produces a much better fold (right).

For book covers, sometimes results can be improved by adding some type of finish to the cover prior to folding. Most documents printed on a digital press can be varnished, laminated, or finished with some type of coating. Usually an aqueous coating or non-oil-based UV coating works best with documents printed using electrophotography. But it is always best to check with the press manufacturer or printer for the recommended coating. If a digitally printed document is going to be mailed, consideration should be given to applying some type of coating as the mailing process can cause unwanted results such as streaking and smearing by the time the mailing gets to its customer.

DESIGNING FOR VARIABLE-DATA PRINTING

Designing for variable-data printing has a few additional considerations in addition to design considerations for static digital printing. All of the design considerations for digital printing apply to VDP as well because VDP is produced using digital printing. Considerations unique to VDP are things such as variable elements, static elements, VDP workflow, database incorporation, imposition, proofing, binding, and finishing.

The design planning for a VDP job can be more intense and time-consuming than planning for static digital printing. There will likely be others involved working on a personalized campaign such as marketing people, designers, printers, and perhaps database specialists. It is important to work with the entire team involved when planning the design of a VDP job. Decisions on varying elements are highly dependent on the database and what information is available. The more that is known about an individual, the more relevant the message is that can be sent to them. It must be decided what elements will be variable and what elements will remain static. It must be decided what varying elements will send an overt message using explicit personalization and what elements will send a covert message using transparent personalization.

A database specialist likely does database management and design. A specialist would determine specific searches and ensure that the data is cleansed and ready for incorporation into a VDP design. It is important to be sure that the data is accurate and conducive to postal regulations and efficiency. Once the database is completed, it is ready to be incorporated into the VDP software application. How the data preparation is done is discussed in more detail in chapter 10.

Because VDP jobs can be more complicated to design, the overall workflow is also more complicated. The VDP workflow consists of a job design, merging, and output (figure 5-14). There may be a variety of people involved in the workflow. The job design includes a database that can have text and graphic elements, a set of rules that determines under what conditions certain elements will be used, static graphic files, and the overall layout. The job is then merged together using some type of VDP software application. Finally, the job is sent to the DFE using some type of VDP output language, and it is then imaged on the marking engine.

Imposition can be a very critical component for VDP output. If something like BRC mailers are being printed and there is variable information on both sides, it is important that one person's front of the mailer match up with their own back of the mailer. Dealing with two-sided printing and multiple-up pages like this imposition can be tricky. Depending on the job flow, the imposition will either be done within the VDP software application or within the DFE. If the VDP software application does the multiple-up layout, it needs to be decided where the two-sided printing will be applied. It may be applied at the DFE. Testing is generally required for each job to determine the proper sequence so the job will print properly.

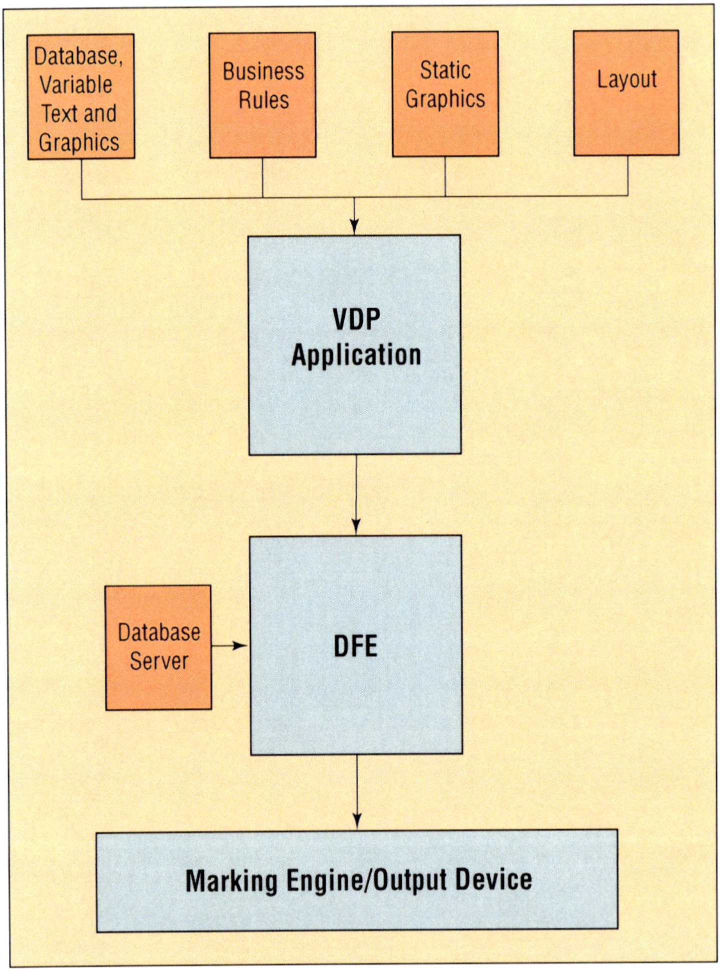

Figure 5-14. *Workflow for variable-data printing.*

Proofing for VDP can be slightly different than proofing for static digital printing. Obviously it isn't possible to print a proof of every record, but it is a good idea to incorporate some soft proofing. Most VDP software applications also have the ability to find the longest and shortest record within each field. This is essential to determine if all the records will fit properly in the designated space. It is still important to generate a contract proof for the customer. This may involve printing more than one proof including things like records with the longest line and prints showing the varying graphic elements. Since VDP design and production is generally more time consuming and costly, accurate proofing and good communication to the client about the varying elements is essential to avoid costly mistakes.

DESIGN TIPS FOR COMBINING DIGITAL AND OFFSET PRINTING

If a project requires that preprinted sheets from an offset press be used in a digital device such as a laser printer, color copier, or digital press, a bright white paper with a smooth finish should be used whenever possible. Toner does not adhere well to uneven paper surfaces, so textured or embossed papers are not recommended. Also, forms preprinted with conventional printing ink tend to smear under the extreme heat and pressure of fuser rollers in high-speed copiers. Ink manufacturers can provide oil-based, wax-formulated, or heat-resistant inks for digital applications. Metallic and fluorescent inks that can flake off and build up on the fuser rollers should be avoided. Toner does not adhere well to heavily inked areas, coatings, or varnishes. The digitally printed image should print directly onto the paper.

The CMYK color gamut of digital printing and offset printing may be different. Therefore, the color gamut of each process should be documented and adjusted to achieve a match.

BINDING, FINISHING, SORTING, AND MAILING

Once a job is printed, there are often steps that need to be done before the job can be delivered. In digital printing, this can be cutting, folding, binding, numbering, diecutting, foil stamping, embossing, laminating, or some other type of protective coating. If the printed piece is a direct mail piece, there may need to be addressing, sorting, or mailing requirements added.

In VDP, where the variable information is printed prior to entering this department, there can be issues related to makeready or waste. Since each piece is unique it isn't feasible to use some up as makeready or to chance that some will get ruined during jams or setups. Therefore, it is important to plan on having extra pieces printed for makeready as needed and also plan on reprinting some pieces if they are ruined at some point in the finishing process. It is important that every person or record within a job receive the piece designed uniquely for them.

The cost of mailing can often times be one of the highest costs in a direct mail campaign. Therefore it is important to understand postal rates and how the best rates possible can apply. The United States Postal Service (USPS) has specific requirements and regulations associated with their bulk rates. It is important to know what these are so the best rates can be used for your client.

It is also important to know at what point a POSTNET barcode should be applied to the piece. A ***POSTNET barcode,*** as shown in figure 5-15, is a barcode needed by the USPS for efficient, automated sorting of the mail. It represents the zip code of the delivery point and automates the sorting to the carrier level by reading the barcode internally at USPS locations. The POSTNET barcode can be added by the VDP software, by a direct mailer during post-press or by the USPS. If the piece is printed completely from a digital press, then it should be added prior to printing. This will save time and money when it comes to mailing the piece.

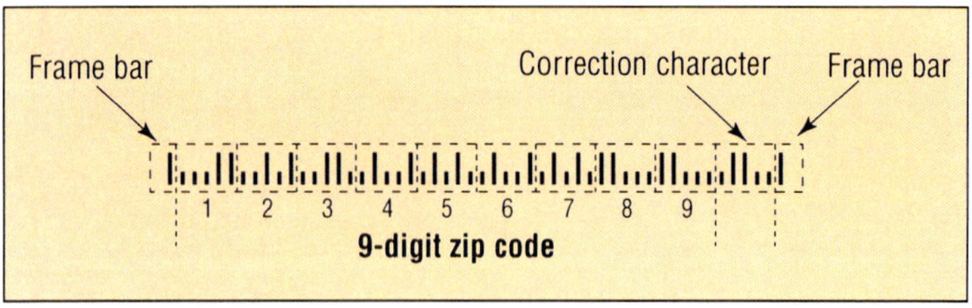

Figure 5-15. *POSTNET barcode.*

6. PostScript and PDF

WHAT IS POSTSCRIPT?

PostScript is a page-description language that allows for the creation of high-quality text and graphics. Every file that is created for print is ultimately output on a PostScript output device. Some examples of PostScript output devices are an imagesetter, a computer-to-plate device (platesetter), a digital color proofing device, and a digital press. Most PostScript output devices have two main components—a ***raster image processor (RIP)*** and a ***marking engine***. In the past, the raster image processor would just rasterize ("rip") files and then send them to the marking engine and nothing more.

Today, RIPs can do many other things along with ripping including color management, imposition, PDF creation, and VDP data merging. These robust RIPs with all the enhanced features are called ***digital front ends (DFEs)***.

The RIP is often a dedicated computer running a particular RIP software. When a file is sent to print it first goes into the RIP to be processed. Located inside the RIP is a PostScript interpreter that reads the PostScript code and converts it to raster data. Adobe's PostScript interpreter is called a ***Configurable PostScript Interpreter (CPSI)*** and is probably the most common PostScript interpreter residing inside various RIPs. The PostScript information is interpreted by the RIP. The RIP takes the PostScript information and converts it to raster data so that the marking engine can then image it. The marking engine images the raster data using spots relative in size to the device's output resolution, which is measured in dots per inch (dpi). An output device with a resolution of 2540 dpi is capable of imaging a much smaller spot than an 600-dpi output device.

PostScript is a code-based language that describes and creates images on a page. PostScript starts creating a page from the lower left corner and uses points as its measurement system. The lines of PostScript code listed on the next page would draw a 1-in. (25.4 mm) square box on a page, as shown in figure 6-1.

```
72 360 moveto
0 72 rlineto
72 0 rlineto
0 -72 rlineto
closepath
stroke
showpage
```

Figure 6-1. A 1-in. square box created using the PostScript code above.

Let's see how this works. From the bottom left of the page the line "72 360 moveto" moves to Point A. Since PostScript uses the point system of measurement, this means Point A is over 1 in. (25.4 mm) and up 5 in. (127 mm). The command "rlineto" in PostScript means "relative line to." So the next line, "0 72 rlineto" moves up 1 in. relative to Point A and arrives at B. The third line, "72 0 rlineto," moves to Point C relative to Point B. Point D is created by the next line, "0 –72 rlineto." The command "closepath" does just that and a PostScript box has been drawn. The box will not show up, however, without the "stroke" command. And finally, the command "showpage" creates the page to display the box. If there were two "showpage" commands, two pages would be created. The PostScript commands on the previous page can be easily tested by simply creating a plain text file which is essentially a basic PostScript file. Adobe Acrobat Distiller can then be used to interpret the PostScript code and create a PDF (Portable Document Format) file with the box rendered onto the page.

WHAT IS PDF?

Adobe developed its PDF format as a means of seamlessly exchanging digital documents between computers within an intranet—and now across the Internet as well. The first version of the software was released in 1992. The software used to create PDF files is ***Adobe Acrobat Distiller,*** and the software used to open ("read") PDF files is ***Adobe Acrobat.*** When the text and graphics become more complicated, PostScript, which has been the *de facto* standard for high-quality output since the mid to late 1980s, can be a relatively complex and redundant language. Because of its complexity, PostScript files can often take a long time to be processed by the RIP. Sometimes the file may not output at all. Sometimes it may crash the RIP, or it may generate a PostScript error. Acrobat Distiller uses the PostScript code and interprets it into a set of object lists and generates a PDF file. The PDF file is less complicated and usually outputs better than PostScript.

HOW DOES DISTILLER WORK?

Acrobat Distiller actually simplifies the PostScript information and removes some of the redundancy inherent in the PostScript language. Distiller has a built in CPSI that interprets the PostScript and then creates raster data and object lists. If a box is drawn on the page, an object list would be created so the box could be plotted and resized without losing quality. A PDF file also contains raster data that allows the image to be viewed on the screen. The end result is a file that can be scaled up and down and can be viewed on the screen. One tremendous advantage of PDF files over their equivalent PostScript files is that they are much smaller. Distiller uses JPEG compression for images and CFF/Type 2 (Compact Font Format) for font compression. PostScript Type 1 fonts are converted to CFF/Type 2 fonts in a PDF file. They are then converted back to Type 1 fonts upon output or when viewing on a screen. A combination of all these factors allows for a smaller file size while maintaining the highest quality.

PDF files can be produced with different levels of compression. This is done through Distiller's Job Options or Adobe PDF Settings. There are pre-defined settings within Distiller, or the settings can be customized for a particular use. If a PDF file is going to be sent or viewed over the Internet, more compression would be required. If it is going to be output on a digital press little to no compression is needed to maintain optimum quality. It is important when creating a PDF file to know what level of compression to use for a particular end-use. (Figures 6-2, 6-3, and 6-4 show the PDF settings used to create the PDFs for this book, which was printed on the Xerox iGen3 Digital Production Press.)

PDF FOR PRINT

PDF files have the ability to embed fonts and graphics. They can be viewed on the screen and they are smaller than their equivalent PostScript file. This makes it an ideal format for use in the printing and publishing industry. Although PDF has been around for some time, the implementation into the print production workflow is still being perfected. New flavors of PDF have arrived on the scene that are better suited for printing and publishing. PDF/X is an acronym for PDF Exchange. PDF/X standards are designed to make the exchange of PDF files more seamless by allowing only certain elements to be contained within a PDF file. For example, PDF files can contain things like audio and video

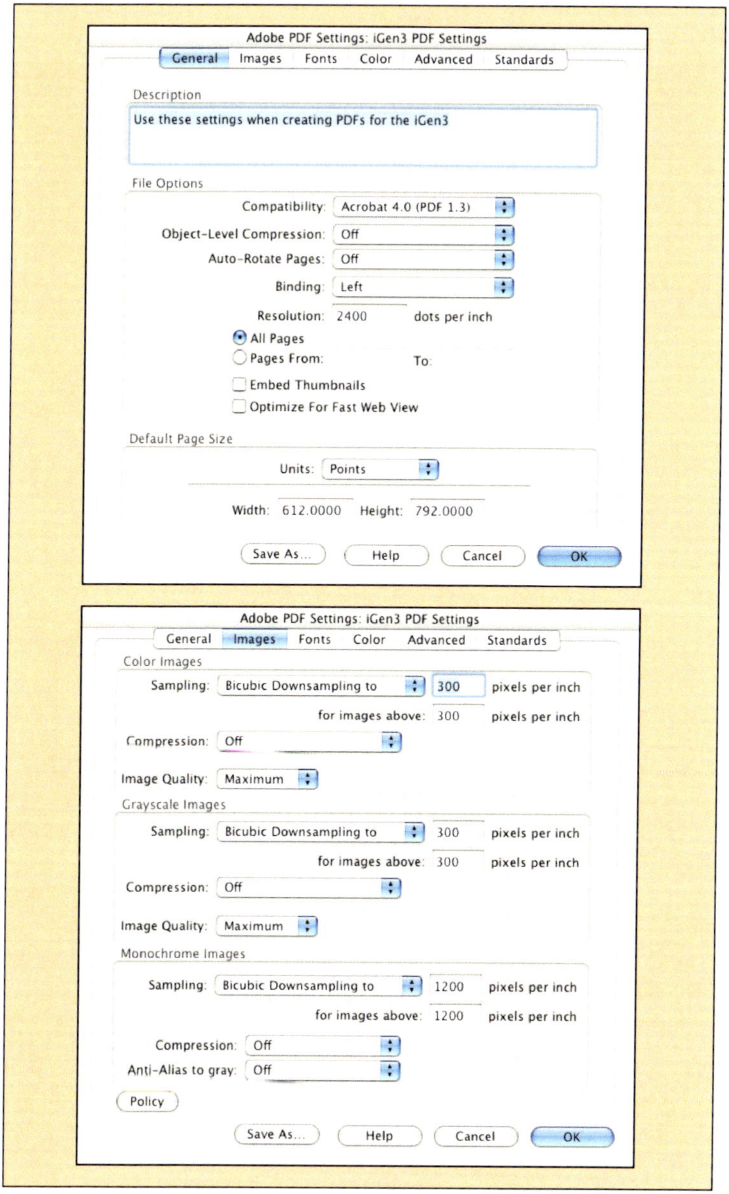

Figure 6-2. *The "General" and "Images" dialog boxes showing Adobe PDF Settings used to print this book.*

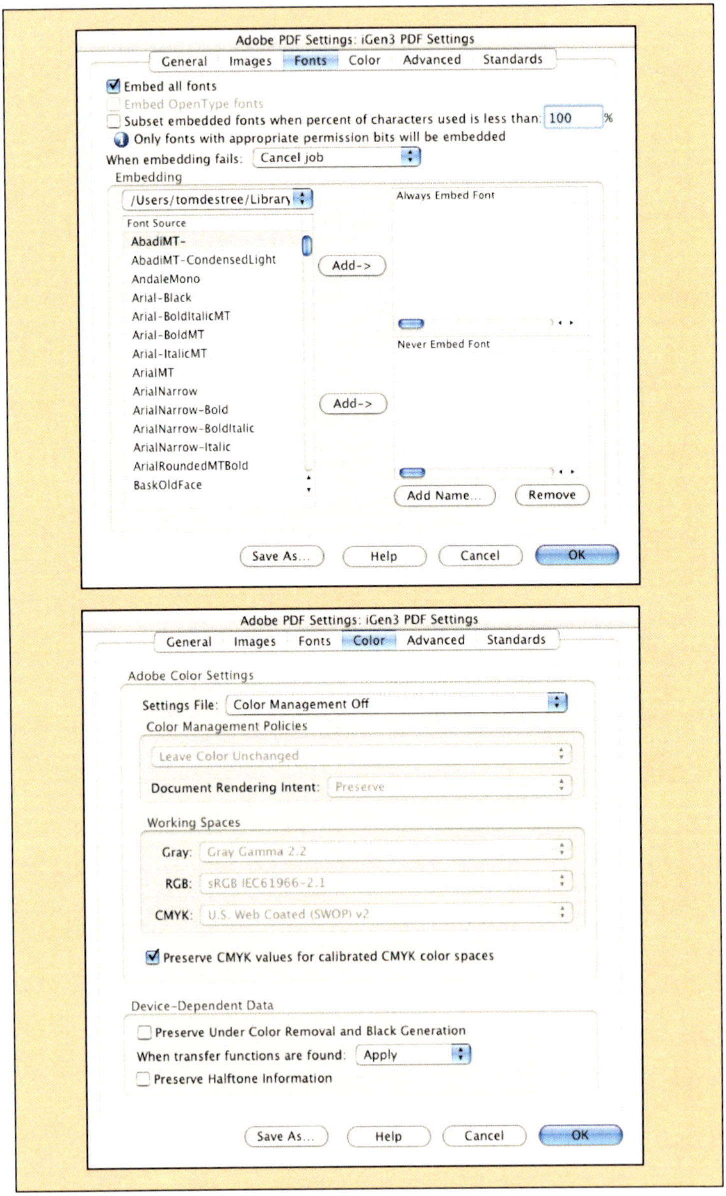

Figure 6-3. *The "Fonts" and "Color" dialog boxes showing Adobe PDF Settings used to print this book.*

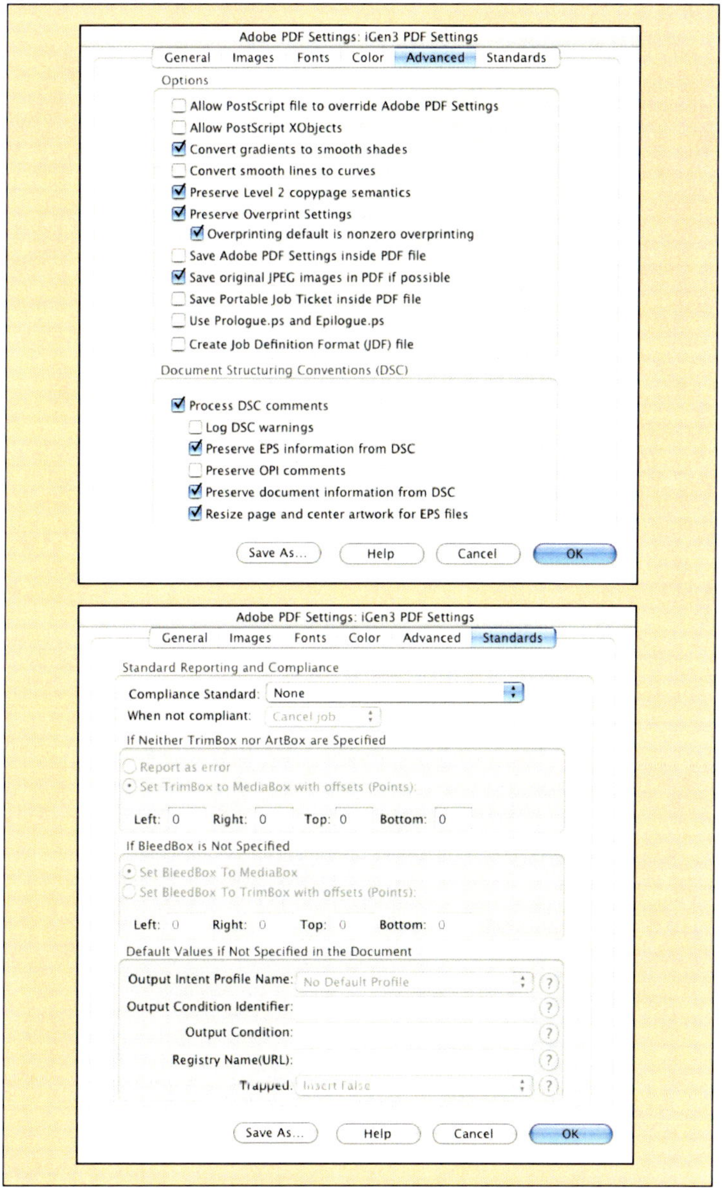

Figure 6-4. *The "Advanced" and "Standards" dialog boxes showing Adobe PDF Settings used to print this book.*

files. However, since PDF files destined for print don't need to contain audio or video, the PDF/X standards restrict the use of those files. The Committee for Graphic Arts Technologies Standards (CGATS) has developed compliance standards for PDF/X-1, PDF/X-1a, PDF/X-2, and PDF/X-3. These standards are essentially a subset of the basic specifications that will ensure PDF files will travel through the print production workflow without problems.

PDF/X-1 and PDF/X-1a both support the complete exchange of CMYK data. The primary difference between PDF/X-1 and PDF/X-1a is that PDF/X-1 allows the file to contain Open Prepress Interface (OPI) while PDF/X-1a does not allow OPI as an option.

PDF/X-2 is designed to enable a "OPI-like" workflow whereas images do not need to be embedded. Unlike the PDF/X-1 standards, device-independent color spaces are allowed. PDF/X-3 supports CMYK data and also supports device-independent color. This format will likely be used in the digital printing world for consistency between digital devices including digital presses.

PREPARING PDF FILES

There are several ways to prepare a PDF file, but it is important to realize that some methods are better than others. PDF files can also be created at different stages of the workflow. It can be created by the content creator, the printer, or blindly within the ripping process. It is best to consult with the printer before submitting a PDF file for output. The most reliable method is a two-step process where PostScript is first written from the native application and then the PostScript data is distilled using Acrobat Distiller. Even though this process is more time consuming, it is the most dependable to ensure proper reproduction of the original layout. PDF files can also be created through a variety of options built into Macintosh OS X. These options should be avoided for files destined to print on a digital press as the results may not reproduce as intended. PDF files can also be generated directly from the application software such as QuarkXPress or InDesign. This is a better option than using the OS X features for PDF creation, but it should be used with caution. It is always best to check with the print provider to determine their recommendations for file submission.

THE FUTURE OF PDF

PDF is better than PostScript as a means to communicate between originator and reproduction device in that it allows for a more compact, yet high-quality, file that generally outputs more efficiently on most RIPs. PDF is very versatile for transmission, proofing, and output of digital files. Trends will continue in future workflows to include PDF as the standard for file preparation and submission. RIPs will soon become PDF-based rather than PostScript-based, which will then encourage the creation of PDF files onto the desktop. Software will then become more efficient at making good PDF files.

7. Digital Printing and VDP Languages and Output Formats

INTRODUCTION TO LANGUAGES AND FORMATS

Languages or output formats specific to digital printing and VDP have emerged along with the evolution of digital presses. Originally, when vendors began developing their digital print engines, most also had proprietary languages or output formats that they developed for efficient output on the print engine. Two common examples still widely used today are Xerox's VIPP and HP Indigo's JLYT. Since the initial development of digital presses and the digital front ends that drive them, there has been tremendous strides in this area.

Defining the Terms "Standard," "Specification," and "Proprietary"

With the advent of the digital era and the ability to create, move, and exchange data so readily, it has brought about a whole host of various languages and formats used for communication and exchange of data. It is important to differentiate between a standard language or format and a specification language or format. A ***standard*** has gone through some type of standards committee such as CGATS or ISO and has been recommended as a standard. A ***specification*** is a specified language or format but has not necessarily been standardized. A standard or specification can be ***open,*** meaning it is available to anyone that wants to develop tools using that particular language or format. Open languages and formats are generally desirable as it creates more opportunity for various vendor tools to communicate and exchange data with one another. ***Proprietary*** languages or formats are developed by a particular company and may not be available for all vendors. Many companies develop vendor partnerships, however, to share proprietary information allowing certain tools to communicate and exchange data with one another. Often times vendors will support and promote their own proprietary language because it has been through several generations of revisions and works well with their particular digital front end (DFE) and/or print engine.

The *defacto* standard for outputting high-quality text and graphics to all digital output devices for over 20 years now has been PostScript. When outputting static jobs, PostScript has remained a great option. But with the introduction of VDP, PostScript alone wasn't an efficient answer. PostScript by its very nature is page-independent and under normal conditions would write separate PostScript code for each page. For VDP though, it just isn't efficient to generate a page for each record within a VDP job. Many of the languages and output formats developed for use in VDP were developed to provide a more efficient method of outputting VDP. It is important to note, though, that the languages and formats discussed in this chapter do not need to be exclusively used for VDP jobs. The proprietary uses of VIPP and JLYT are much broader than just an option for VDP.

As digital presses began to develop further and as software manufacturers began offering design tools for VDP, there became a need to develop open languages and formats for data exchange between vendors. Open standards and specifications available today are Personalized Print Markup Language (PPML) and Personalized Print Markup Language/Variable Data Exchange (PPML/VDX).

It is important to understand the relationship between the content creation software, whether it be static or VDP, and the DFE receiving the file, as shown in figure 7-1. There must be compatibility between the two. The VDP software is the "producer," and the DFE is the "consumer." The exchange between the producer and the consumer must be compatible. For example, if a certain software generates PPML/VDX but a certain DFE will not

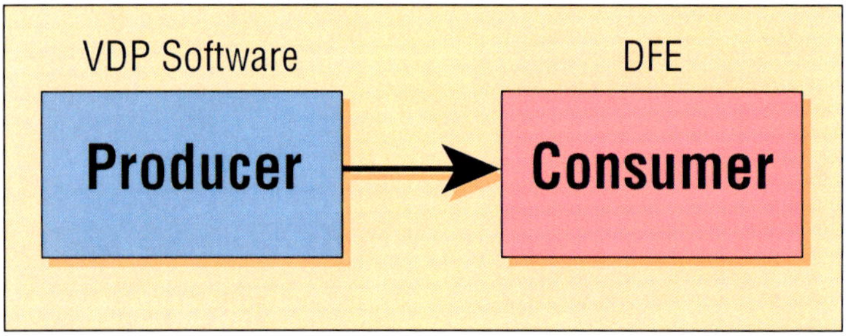

Figure 7-1. *The relationship between the content creation software, whether it be static or VDP, and the DFE receiving the file.*

consume that particular format, then there is a problem. Many software vendors allow for a large variety of output options, but not all DFEs will take in all formats.

Proprietary formats. HP Indigo's J-Layout (JLYT), sometimes also known as Jay Layout, is an output format originally developed by the Indigo team of developers and is now still strongly supported as the proprietary format for all HP Indigo digital presses. It isn't an output language but it is a print job layout and control specification unique to HP Indigos. It works by creating a container for putting information into such as page information, various elements such as images, personalized data or other workflow enhancements such as imposition templates. HP Indigo presses accept JLYT format as well as the standard PPML format into their print stream.

Another proprietary format is Xerox's Variable-Data Intelligent PostScript Printware (VIPP). VIPP (figure 7-2) has be around since 1992 and is considered a macro programming language based on PostScript. VIPP is similar to JLYT in that it merges a variety of data into one consistent format. VIPP is used not only for VDP, but also for data exchange across networks and within intranets.

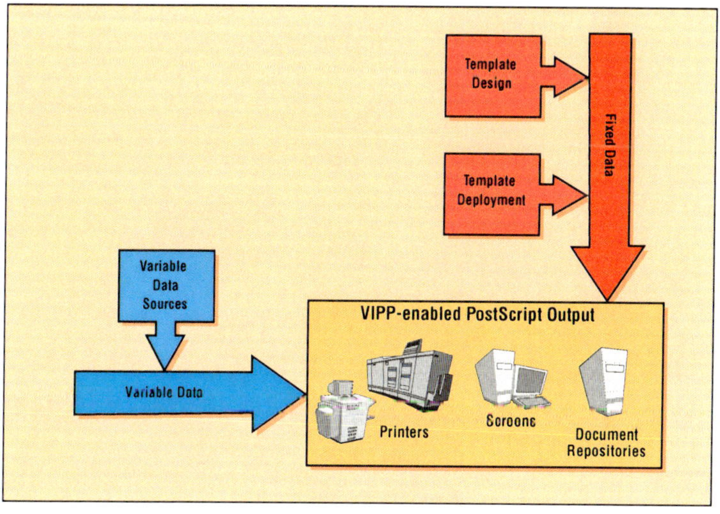

Figure 7-2. Preparing (vertical axis) and running (horizontal axis) variable-data jobs in a VIPP workflow. (Courtesy Xerox)

Languages/formats based on standards and specifications. ***Personalized Print Markup Language (PPML)*** is a specification that was originally developed and released in March 2000 by a group called the Print On Demand initiative (PODi). PPML was designed as an open industry language based on the ***Extensible Markup Language (XML).*** The idea behind PPML was to develop a language for VDP that was not vendor-specific. Prior to this, vendors had developed their own proprietary language for VDP output. Initially, the problem was that vendors already had developed proven languages that worked quite efficiently on their RIPs. At the time PPML was being developed some of the vendors were in their second or third generation of language development. They had a proven language that worked very well on their system. PPML then had some catching up to do. They've tried to do just that.

PPML specifications were updated in 2002 to be more efficient for digital output, but also to incorporate digital job ticketing information with the use of Job Definition Format (JDF). JDF is discussed in more detail later.

Personalized Print Markup Language/Variable Data Exchange (PPML/VDX) was first published in 2002 by the Committee for Graphic Arts Technologies Standards (CGATS), a committee of the American National Standards Institute (ANSI). Since that time it has also been adopted as an International Organization for Standardization (ISO) digital data format. This is significant because it is now an international standard. It allows for open data exchange across individuals, vendors, and platforms. PPML/VDX is a combination of PPML version 2.1 and PDF version 1.4. It combines the benefits of both PDF and PPML technology. It also is compatible with JDF and allows for digital job ticketing information.

SPECIAL NEEDS FOR OUTPUTTING VDP

VDP requires a unique type of processing. If each unique page were to be rasterized (ripped) separately as in a traditional graphic arts workflow, the processing time would be enormous. Output languages and formats designed to output VDP rasterize (rip) the static information once and store it at the RIP and then rip just the variable information for each page. This can be thought of similarly to the use of ***open prepress interface (OPI)*** in graphic arts workflows. OPI would store high-resolution graphics data on a server located close by the RIP to reduce the amount of network traffic. With increased networks speeds, OPI isn't used as much any more but the concepts are similar with VDP output.

Presumably a VDP job will have both static and variable information. The most efficient output then would be to rip the static information and store it as post-ripped data on the DFE and then rip only the variable information as needed. All output languages and formats discussed in this chapter use this type of efficiency with VDP.

THE NEED FOR AUTOMATION

The ***Job Definition Format (JDF)*** is an XML-based open standard format that is housed by the International Cooperation for the Integration of Processes in Prepress, Press and Postpress Organization (CIP4). JDF can be viewed as an enabling technology that allows a communication or handshake between various vendor tools throughout the print production process. JDF can be used for exchanging data from content creator into the printing company's management information system (MIS). The data exchange can then take place between prepress and into press and postpress.

The concept behind more automation and easier exchange of data is a good one. The printing industry requires a great deal of human intervention in its production process and by most manufacturing standards is not that automated, yet. JDF and other technologies will help streamline and automate print production, especially in the area of digital printing. With the short runs and quick turnaround times needed for digital printing, more automation is in high demand. Vendors have been working on an enabling technology that works in conjunction with JDF and is targeted towards digital printers. It is ***Universal Printer Pre and Post-Processing Interface (UP3I),*** which is an open specification that allows for a wide variety of devices to interface together, regardless of the manufacturer. JDF and UP3I work harmoniously together in the workflow. JDF describes the job-related parameters while UP3I controls the print and finishing processes. Together they help automate the digital printing workflow from content creation to finished product.

8. Output Technologies

When you say "digital printer" you are covering a great deal of ground, from very low-end desktop devices to color-based devices that compete with printing presses. Digital printing is based on a variable image carrier—or rather the need to re-image each page for each copy—unlike a printing press image carrier which is fixed and therefore reproduces multiple copies without changing. This variability, based on re-imaging, leads us to two outcomes that cannot be accomplished conventionally: variable-data printing and on-demand publications. You cannot make each sheet different on a printing press. If you do, something is wrong.

Making each sheet different lets you produce personalized or customized sheets that add information about me, to me, for me, concerning me—me, the most important person in my life. You can also output each page of a document in the proper order so as to produce a paginated publication on demand. The dream of on-demand books finally becomes a reality.

You could integrate an inkjet system at the back end of the press, but it is not the same as making every sheet different. You could also preprint the color and static areas of a document and then imprint the variable data on a black-and-white digital printer. But, to produce full-color variable-data printing, where both text and images are personalized to the recipient, you need a digital printing system, and right now that means toner or inkjet printing in black-and-white and color.

OVERVIEW OF REPLICATION TECHNOLOGIES

The defining devices of paper-based replication are:

- Printer
- Copier
- Press

A printer uses inkjet, thermal, wax-transfer, or toner technology to make marks on paper from data files, resulting in the production of first-generation originals where every one of them can be different, thus allowing the production of a collated document or individual, personalized impressions.

A copier uses inkjet or toner technology to make marks on paper from an original, resulting in the production of a second-generation copy, which, when copying multiple originals in an automatic document handler, can also produce a collated document.

A press typically means a mechanical device that uses an image carrier to replicate the same image on paper, over and over again, resulting in a large quantity of the same images. A press may also handle larger sheets, resulting in multiple pages on one large sheet of paper used in a binding/finishing operation.

In 1995, International Data Corp. reported that the number of pages printed on printers for the first time exceeded pages printed on all models of copying machines. This led Hewlett-Packard to coin a new buzzword: ***mopier***—a multiple-original printer. If you make multiple-original prints from an original-producing printer instead of an original-copying copier, it is a mopier. Since copiers are evolving to digital approaches—scanners on the top and printers on the bottom—they become de facto printers.

Printers at every level are challenging offset duplication at the low end of the black-and-white printing world. Low-end printers are absorbing some of the work of both offset duplicators and mid-level copiers. As scanners become cheaper and wind up on virtually every desktop, we can easily scan hard copy and print when we want to actually make a copy. But in most cases we are already preparing the information in computers and will probably print that information on a printer, rather than make one print and then copy it.

Levels of Replication Devices

Most files that would have been printed out and then copied are now just printed out in the required quantity. So over time we arrive at the following levels of replication devices:

- Printer (dynamic imaging)
- Printer-press (digital press or digital duplicator or production printer)
- Scanner-printer (digital copier)
- Press (static image carrier)

A printer connects to a computer, big or small, and prints on paper at speeds from 1 to 100 pages per minute, simplex (that is, printing one side of the sheet). They range from desktop printers to production printers, increasing in the volume they can produce in a month (duty cycle) and usually in quality. A printer-press is the way we presently describe a high-end black-and-white or color printer. In order to provide the production speed, these devices have had to find innovative methods for moving paper.

Using rollers may provide opportunities for jams, so belts are used which hold the paper on them with static electricity. Or, webs (rolls) of paper are used. It may be that instead of re-imaging the photoconductive drum or belt for each copy, we image it once for some number of copies or even for all copies. Lastly, we are seeing the sheet size increase so that more pages are imaged at one time. These devices then become high-speed, high-capability printers and usually integrate some level of on-line bindery and finishing.

A scanner-printer is a printer with a scanner somewhere in the system, usually built into the device. These devices most often have plugs for network connectivity through an optional raster image processor (RIP). Calling them copiers makes no sense, but the term will persist for a long time.

A press is just what it is now, with plates and ink, printing a number of pages of the same information, on a large sheet of paper. Press refers to a device that makes an image carrier and then replicates images from that carrier. Every image is the same (hopefully). Think printing press when you think press. The term "digital press" attempts to cover very high-end printers.

Static Printing vs. Dynamic (Variable) Printing

The reproduction of information on paper falls into two categories: static printing and dynamic printing.

Static printing refers to traditional ink-on-paper approaches, offset lithography being the most common, where each and every sheet is reproduced from the same image carrier which is fixed with the same image. The copies look exactly the same. Toner-based printers, conversely, use an image carrier that is imaged each time a sheet comes in contact with it, re-imaging for each copy. The copies look the same, but each is generated individually. ***Dynamic printing*** means that the printer must re-generate the image for every page; thus, every page can be different, which then allows for *variable-data printing*. Table 8-1 compares static printing with dynamic, or variable-data, printing.

Table 8-1. Process Differences between Static Printing and Dynamic Printing

	Static (offset printing)	Dynamic (digital printing)
Image carrier	Fixed	Variable
Material	Ink	Toner, Inkjet
Quality	High	Moderate++
Variability	None	High
Quantities	Moderate to high >2000	Low to moderate <2000
Paper selection	High	Limited to moderate
Sheet size	Small to large	Small to some medium
Documents	Moderate to long runs	Short to some moderate runs

The advantage to static printing is the cost-effectiveness of long runs. You can actually plot the relationship between offset color printing and digital color printing by comparing run length and cost per unit. Our numbers have always shown that offset printing has a high up-front cost based on makeready and that each additional unit printed absorbs a part of that cost. The more units, the less cost per unit. Digital printing on the other hand has no makeready as such, and each unit costs the same.

The advantage of dynamic printing is that the re-imaging for each sheet lets you do two things you cannot do with a printing press:

- Each sheet personalized to a person or company
- One multipage document at a time

You can only do these things on a digital printer. There are some other advantages but, in some cases, newer printing presses with built-in automation compete in the areas of:

- Very short runs
- Very fast turnaround
- Distributed printing

Nonimpact Printers

The output devices used in today's digital printers trace their lineage back to the first nonimpact printers that were attached to early computers. ***Nonimpact printers*** were developed as an alternative to the original impact typewriter and dot matrix devices to provide faster printout speeds, larger character sets, and more fonts. They were called "nonimpact printers" because, theoretically, there is no contact between the printer and substrate—although ink or toner transfer to the substrate must of necessity involve some contact. The ***impact printers*** of that time housed characters on belts and wheels and were too slow, broke down often, and could not produce high resolution.

Today, three primary technologies are used with nonimpact/digital printers: inkjet, thermal (thermal transfer, dye sublimation), and electrophotography (toner).

In general, nonimpact printers create images by *gently* placing spots on the page—otherwise they would be *impact printers!* The print engine provides control of dot size and dot placement. With electrophotography, the laser is aimed at the imaging target with a fixed rate and beam size. With inkjet, the print head controls the drop rate and size. The method of creating lines, characters, and graphic images are the same in both types of printers.

ELECTROPHOTOGRAPHY

The electrophotographic process (figure 8-1) is a well-established process used in a variety of laser printing, copying devices, and digital printing presses. (The discussion that follows is a representative example of the process. The exact mechanism of image creation and transfer varies somewhat by manufacturer.) There are five basic steps:

1. **Cleaning.** The left-over electrical charges from the previous image are removed from the ***organic photoconductor (OPC)*** surface using a light source (in corona-based engines) and toner is removed from the OPC by the wiper blade.
2. **Conditioning or charging.** An even charge is applied to the OPC using a corona wire or ***primary charge roller (PCR)*** with a negative surface charge. If the corona wire fails to

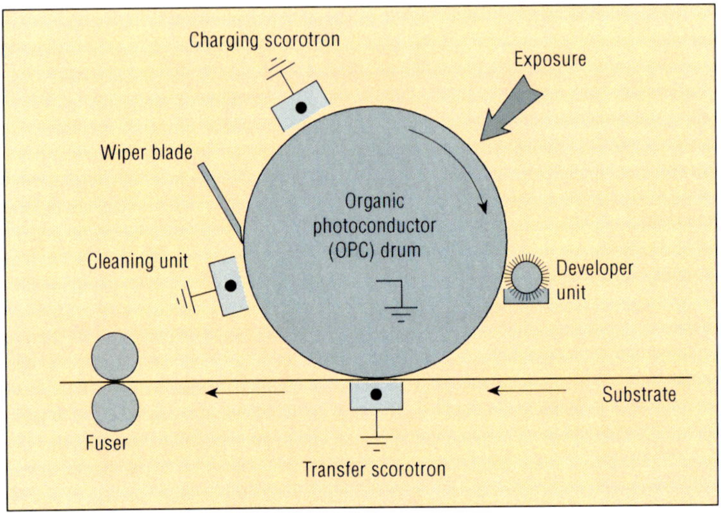

Figure 8-1. *The operating principle of an electrophotographic digital press.*

completely recharge the drum, ***positive image ghosting*** could occur, which is caused by toner transferring to those portions of the latent image remaining on the OPC drum.

3. **Writing (imaging) or discharging.** Specific areas of the drum are exposed to ***laser*** or ***light-emitting diode (LED)*** light which reduces the charge in those areas, forming a latent image. During this process, the light activates electron pairs in the ***charge generating layer (CGL).*** These electron pairs separate and migrate to both the aluminum substrate and the surface of the ***charge transport layer (CTL).*** Both the aluminum substrate and the CTL charges become neutral. (The OPC is discussed in detail later in this section.)

   Since no toner is yet distributed to the drum, the image is called a ***latent,*** or potential, ***image.*** Only after the developer roller transfers the toner to the OPC drum does it become a visible image. After the toner is transferred to the paper and the nontransferred toner is removed by the wiper blade, the latent image remains on the OPC drum—which is why the cleaning and conditioning steps are so important.

4. **Developing.** Toner is applied to the discharged areas of the drum using a magnetic roller, or a developer roller, and are electrically attracted to the photoconductive drum.

   The toner cartridge releases the toner and the magnetized carrier particles from a magnetic brush pass down the drum, transferring toner particles that adhere to the latent electrostatic image on the drum.

5. **Transferring toner to paper.** As the sheet or web of paper passes the OPC, the toner is transferred from the OPC surface onto the paper using an oppositely-charged electric field and gravity.

   After the image is transferred to the paper, it is fused to the paper with heat. The fusing process is accomplished by the ***fuser,*** or ***fixing assembly,*** in the printer. The Xeikon print engine, for example, uses a non-contact radiant fusing system.

OPC Technology

The building block of electrophotographic technology is the ***organic photoconductor (OPC),*** which consists of an aluminum core covered with a light-sensitive material, selenium for example, that converts light energy into an electrical charge. OPCs are also referred to as ***drums,*** because of their cylindrical shape, but many are also belts. Many drums have a large drive gear on one side and the electrical input/output contacts on the other. Some OPCs have conductive gears.

The main function of an OPC is to transfer toner to specific areas of the page. During development, the OPC is involved in the five stages just described—cleaning, conditioning or charging, writing (imaging) or discharging, developing, and transfer.

The base material is usually made out of an anodized aluminum alloy. Its coating consists of a charge generating layer (CGL) and a charge transport layer (CTL). The CGL is usually 0.2–0.5 microns thick. The CGL consists mainly of an organic photoconductor, a semiconducting organic chemical that releases electrons (allowing current to flow) when exposed to light. The active chemical is in the hydrazine family, a cousin to rocket fuel.

Organic photoconductors predominate over inorganic because of environmental reasons. Inorganic chemicals may work better, but most are extremely toxic and would be hazardous waste. OPCs are not toxic and may be safely disposed of in a sanitary landfill.

The CTL is a polymer (plastic resin), often polycarbonate, and is 15–35 microns thick. Because the OPC must be in constant contact with the wiper blade, abrasive papers, toner, and charge roller, the hard plastic CTL protects the surface of the OPC from quickly wearing down to the CGL. The CTL is also laced with a photoconductive chemical so that charges can transfer smoothly through the polymer layer without causing an arc, which would produce erratic prints. Without light, the overall coating is an insulator, similar to the plastic coating on an electrical cord, but very thin. The charge applied by the PCR stays on the surface of the coating and does not travel to the ground because the coating acts as an insulator.

When a spot on the OPC is imaged with light energy from the laser or LED, the light travels through the clear polymer coating to the charge generating layer. The CGL absorbs some of the energy and temporarily releases electrons at that spot. When that happens, most of the charge at that spot on the surface immediately conducts (or leaks) through the CTL to the active CGL, and out through the drum substrate to the ground. The activated coating still has a little resistance and the residual charge on a discharged portion of the OPC only drops to 100 to 200 volts, instead of 0.

The unimaged area of the photoconductor surrounding the active spot still acts as an insulator, so the charge is insulated from the ground. Otherwise all of the charge would leak out, and only black pages would print. The resulting electrical field looks something like a funnel that curves out. During the development stage, the toner is pushed onto the funnel and adheres to the surface of the polymer. Toner is repelled from the surrounding areas that have a full –600 to –700 volt charge.

OPC drums vary in both electrical and physical characteristics. Dark printing OPCs are referred to as "hot," and light printing OPCs as "cold." The difference between the hot and cold OPC is the level of sensitivity to the laser beam (the activation of electron carriers), and the time frame in which the OPC surface will hold the neutralized hole. A hot OPC will have more electrons activated when the laser beam strikes the OPC surface and holds the higher charge for a longer time period. A cooler OPC will have fewer electrons activated and the charge will drop more rapidly.

Drum wear. Many factors determine the life cycle of an OPC drum. Surface wear of the CTL, for example, is usually a factor of the wiper blade and PCR due to friction and heat. The wear varies depending on what type of machine is being used and the nature of the substrate. Another factor that comes into play regarding wear is the diameter of the drum. A larger diameter means fewer revolutions and, therefore, less wear.

Wiper Blade

The ***wiper blade,*** or ***cleaning blade,*** removes the untransferred toner from the OPC drum so it can be recharged and used again. All wiper blades are made of urethane and are attached to a metal frame. They are either glued or molded to the frame but essentially they all work in the same manner. The leading corner of the blade is the only part that comes into contact with the OPC drum. Because of the friction between the OPC drum and the leading edge of the blade, poorly lubricated blades often cause the edge of the blade to flip upwards. This condition is known as a ***wiper blade flip.*** A wiper blade failure is usually indicated by a thin vertical line on the page. The only solution is to replace the wiper blade.

Doctor Blade

The ***doctor blade/bar,*** also known as a ***metering blade/bar,*** serves two distinct purposes:

- It gives toner a triboelectric charge which aids in the development stage of the electrophotographic process
- It measures the distribution of toner on the developer roller.

Most are made of metal with a urethane edge, but some are just made of steel. They are used to maintain an even layer of toner on the developer roller regardless of the material that the developer roller is made of. Cartridges with multiple cycles often show a wear spot in the urethane of the doctor blade where it was in contact with the developer roller. The job of the blade is to keep a nice even layer of toner on the developer roller.

Life Expectancy of Consumables

There is no exact answer to how long consumables will last. Whether OPCs, wiper blades, or other consumables, there are too many variables to give exact numbers. The number of pages printed by the same amount of toner can vary greatly from cycle to cycle. Page counts alone are not the only determining factor in wear. The components themselves, working in conjunction with each other, can increase or decrease wear:

- Some toners are more abrasive than others leading to higher drum wear.
- A wiper blade that may still be cleaning properly might cause excessive drum wear if it has become brittle from aging. Proper lubrication is also a must to reduce wear as much as possible.
- Worn mag sleeve bushings can contribute to premature drum wear.

These are just a few examples of the many variables that can affect wear. It is these many factors, some controllable and some not, that make it impossible to nail down exact life expectancy numbers. Although specific guaranteed numbers cannot be given, general expectations under average operating conditions certainly can.

If that layer starts to become too thick, print defects will start to show up. These defects include poor character fill due to increased pile height of the toner, backgrounding, and leakage from the toner hopper of the cartridge. In some cases the toner will build up on the developer roller to the point that not all of it will pass the mylar strip behind the developer roller and leakage will result.

Three types of doctor blades/bars are found in the most popular toner cartridges. The original metering device was a bar type held in place with screws. The screws could adjust the metering bar to increase or decrease the amount of toner released on the developer roller. A second type of blade consists of a polyurethane blade that is either glued or molded to a metal stamping. Another type of blade is made of an aluminum material with a soft, pliable, rubberized type of backing. The backing is glued to a metal stamping that has foam on each end to help prevent leakage.

Several print defects will occur with a bad or worn doctor blade/bar. ***Backgrounding*** or uneven print is a common defect.

Although these bars can be used for a number of cycles before becoming worn, print defects such as light print, side-to-side print variations, and backgrounding will appear as the blade wears. A common problem associated with a worn doctor blade is referred to as ***tire tracks,*** which appears as wavy lines running down the page. In this case, the wavy pattern will also show up on the magnetic developer roller. In other cartridges, a worn doctor blade may cause improper charging of toner, resulting in light print.

Fusing

Fusing or fixing causes toner to adhere to itself and to the printed page. The fuser's main components are:

- The heating element (lamp)
- Upper roller (film)
- Lower roller
- Thermistor (heat sensor)
- Thermoswitch (safety circuit)

The thermistor will sense when the fuser element has reached optimum temperature, prompting a ready message. The thermistor will continuously regulate the operation of the heating element, turning it on and off as necessary to keep the temperature within range. The element itself is located inside the upper fuser roller which is responsible for the actual fusing once it is heated by the element. The lower roller, also referred to as the pressure roller, applies pressure to the paper and image forcing them against the upper fuser roller which adheres the image to the page.

Problems may interfere with the fusing process: a worn upper roller (which causes toner build-up), worn pressure springs (which fail to press the lower roller against the upper roller), or a damaged gear. A toner-based system is an interesting blend of mechanical, electronic, and other elements.

REPRESENTATIVE ELECTROPHOTOGRAPHIC OUTPUT DEVICES

Most of the output devices used for digital printing operate on the electrophototographic principles just discussed. The following discussion provides an overview of a few of these systems. Since the technology and products change so frequently, the reader is advised to contact the various manufacturers or visit their websites to obtain current product offerings and detailed product descriptions. In most instances, the manufacturer offers more models than those listed below.

Canon imagePRESS C7000VP. The imagePRESS C7000VP (figure 8-2) from Canon U.S.A. (www.usa.canon.com), announced in early 2006, prints at 70 pages per minute (ppm) for letter-sized output in color and black-and-white. It uses Canon's new-generation color imagePlatform controller, Gloss Optimization technology, and improved toner to deliver job-to-job, day-to-day, week-to-week color consistency designed to rival offset quality printing.

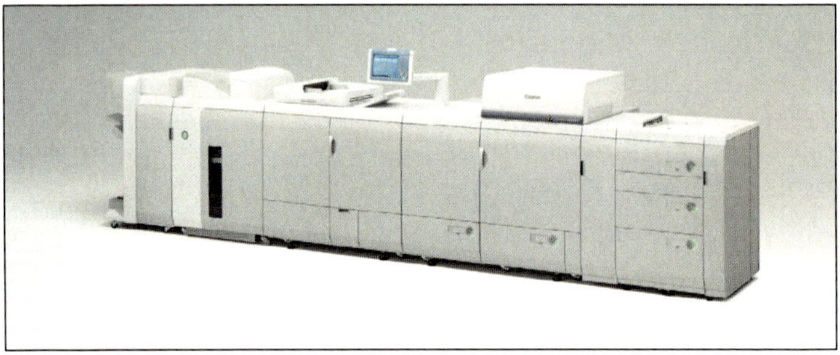

Figure 8-2. *Canon imagePRESS C7000VP. (Courtesy Canon U.S.A.)*

The imagePRESS C7000VP incorporates a new V-Toner, new T-Developer and new E-Drum in conjunction with an oil-less fusing system. New high-precision registration systems and imaging control technologies allow the engine to run at rated speeds on substrates up to 300 grams per square meter (gsm). To integrate with existing workflows and methods, the engine is driven by a new imagePRESS Server A3000 controller that was co-developed with Electronics for Imaging (EFI). The imagePRESS C7000VP has a 10,000-sheet air-assisted paper feeding capacity and offers online finishing that includes high-capacity stacking, punching, trimming, and saddle-stitched booklet making.

HP Indigo press 5000. Hewlett Packard (www.hp.com) offers both sheetfed and rollfed (web) digital printing solutions. The HP Indigo press 5000 (figure 8-3) is a sheetfed digital press that uses a

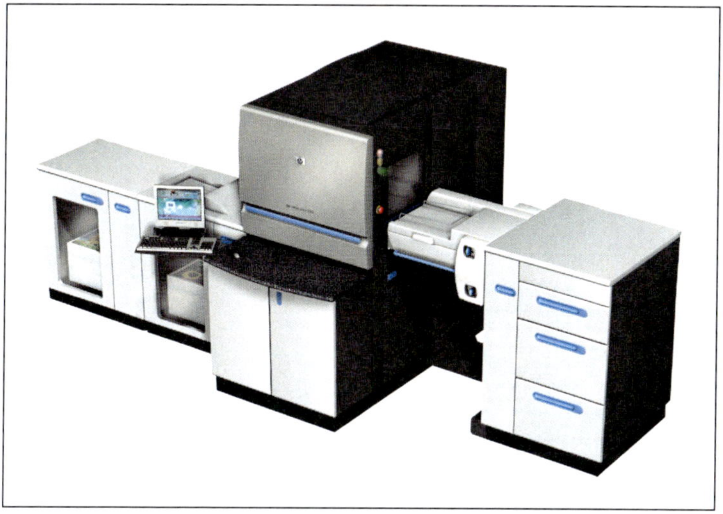

Figure 8-3. HP Indigo press 5000. (Courtesy Hewlett-Packard)

liquid ink technology, called ***ElectroInk.*** This patented process creates high-definition imaging and sharp text—at 812×812 dpi and up to 812×1624 dpi when in high-resolution mode and halftones up to 230 lines per inch (lpi).

Many of the traditional parts of electrophotographic engines are not present in the HP Indigo series. A PIP, or electroplate, is charged and receives the color spots. These are transferred to a blanket. The blanket is heated and the image is transferred to paper or other substrates. Thus, fusing is not required.

Five-, six-, and seven-color inking stations augment the four process colors with HP IndiChrome colors to expand the color gamut. In addition, the new HP Indigo Digital Matte ink creates a differential gloss effect that adds a spot varnish look.

The press has throughput speeds of 4,000 four-color 8.5×11-in. images per hour (two-up), 8,000 two-color or single-color 8.5×11-in. images per hour (two-up), and 16,000 full monochrome 8.5×11-in. images per hour.

The HP Indigo w3250. The webfed HP Indigo press w3250 (figure 8-4) combines the quality of offset printing with the flexibility of digital printing and also features inline finishing capabilities.

Figure 8-4. *HP Indigo press w3250. (Courtesy Hewlett-Packard)*

Two print engines deliver 4,000 duplex 8.5×11.5-in. four-color images per hour or 8,000 duplex one-color or two-color pages, in roll-to-roll or roll-to-sheet. The press supports a wide range of substrates—from lightweight media required for books and manuals to heavier substrates required for postcards. The press has a standard resolution of 800×800 dpi and prints at 800×1600 dpi in high-resolution mode, and it can print halftones up to 230 lpi.

The press can print in full process color as well as up to three spot colors in a single pass and, like other HP Indigo presses, uses ElectroInk.

IBM Infoprint 4100 Advanced Function Printing System. IBM (www.printers.ibm.com) offers the broad line of Infoprint 4100 printers (figure 8-5), which includes eight models designed to meet a variety of enterprise and commercial printing needs. The HD5/HD6, the fastest model in the Infoprint 4100 line, can print at up to 330 linear feet (100.6 m) per minute, which is 1,440 two-up duplex letter impressions or 1,354 two-up duplex A4 impressions).

The machines support the use of both pin-fed and pinless paper (preprinted, plain, boxed fanfold forms, and roll-feed paper) in a variety of weight ranges depending on the model. Pin-fed paper width ranges from 8.3 to 19.5 in. (210 mm to 495 mm), and pinless paper width ranges from 8 to 19.5 in. (203 mm to 495 mm). The maximum pin-fed print width is 18.5 in. (469 mm), and the maximum pinless print width is 19 in. (482 mm).

Figure 8-5. *IBM Infoprint 4100 Advanced Function Printing System. (Courtesy IBM)*

Kodak NexPress 2100 Plus Digital Production Press. Kodak Graphic Communications Group (http://graphics.kodak.com/) offers the NexPress 2100 (figure 8-6), a sheetfed design that allows the user to choose from a wide range of paper stocks and mix up to three different papers in a single job. The NexPress 2100 is designed with three separate on-line feeders that give operators the flexibility to change or add papers while printing, and these feeders offer a total pile height of 26 in. (650 mm). The NexPress 2100 handles paper sizes up to 13.8×18.5 in. (350×470 mm) with weights from 20-lb. bond to 110-lb. cover (80–300 gsm). The NexPress uses DryInk™ technology, giving the user the flexibility to proceed directly to finishing, and electronic collation allows the user to easily produce fully completed, ready-to-bind printed products.

The NexPress 2100 employs a near-line finishing approach that provides flexibility in finishing. With the specially designed main delivery it is easy to transfer jobs to complex folding, perfect binding, mechanical binding, booklet making, backstitching, and cutting machines.

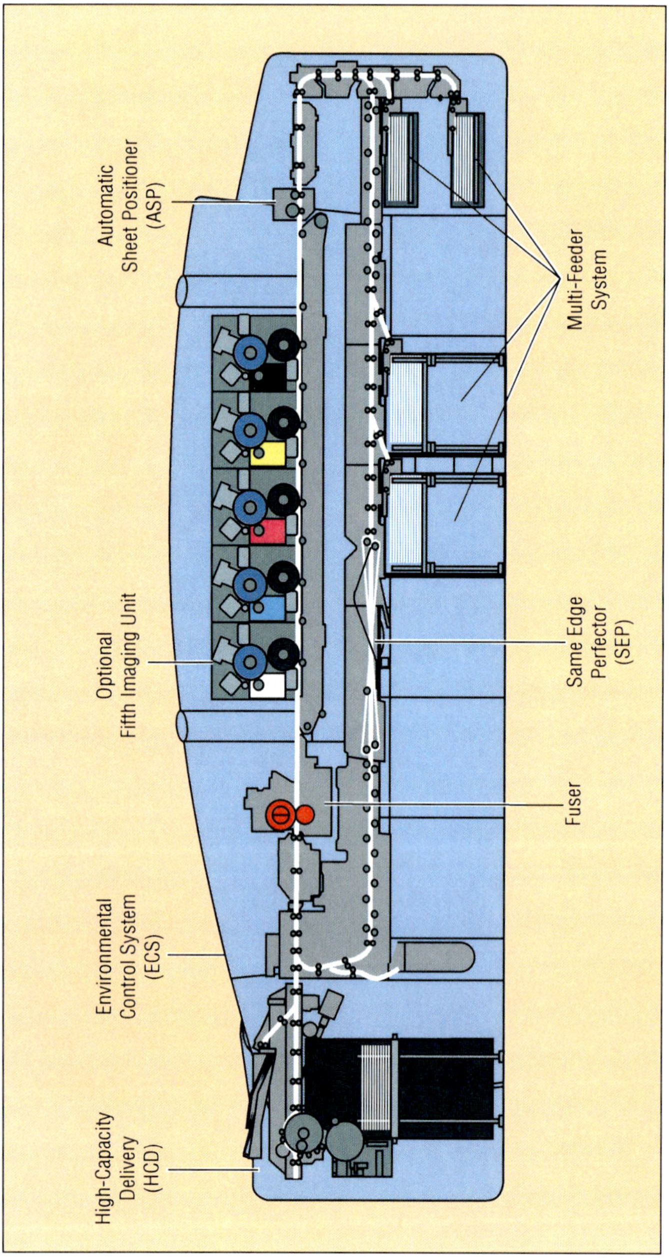

Figure 8-6. *Kodak NexPress 2100 digital color production press. (Courtesy Kodak Graphic Communications Group)*

Xeikon 5000. Xeikon (www.xeikon.com), a brand of Punch Graphix, offers a webfed digital printing solution—the Xeikon 5000 (figure 8-7), which is unique in its handling of paper widths of 500 mm with virtually no restriction in sheet length. Ready to print the longest jobs on a wide range of paper stocks, it can also print on a wide choice of other substrates such as polyester film, transfer material, and label stock from 40 to 350 gsm, adding a wide assortment of value-generating applications. The Xeikon 5000 can print multipage documents at a speed of 7,800 full-color pages per hour, which translates into 130 A4 pages per minute in fully collated order.

The Xeikon has a 600-dpi output resolution with every dot capable of variable density levels. As a standard, the Xeikon 5000 comes equipped with an in-line densitometer, ensuring front-to-back register, color register, and color consistency throughout the pressrun.

The Xeikon 5000 comes integrated with the X-800 Digital Front-End (DFE) system, which embeds powerful streamer technology that yields new levels of high-end variable-data printing. This open, scalable, and modular system combines powerful RIP features with print quality tools and collation capabilities. In addition, it allows simultaneous setup, ripping, and printing of a

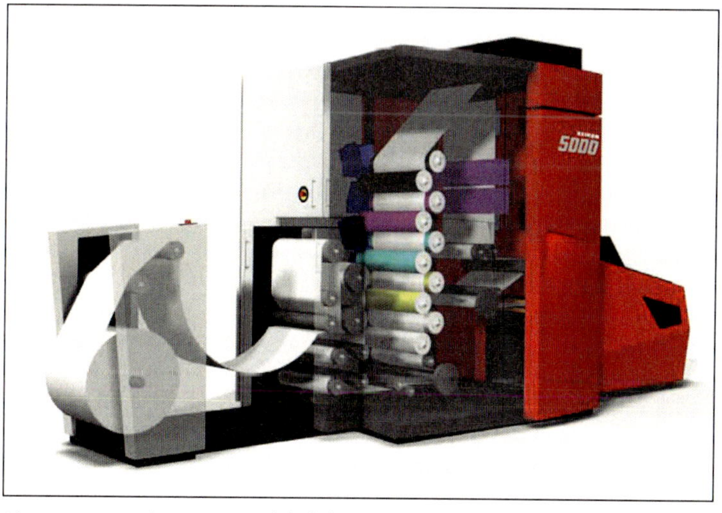

Figure 8-7. Xeikon 5000 webfed digital press. (Courtesy Punch Graphix)

file. The X-800 DFE easily processes PostScript, PDF, PPML, and PPML/VDX files at high speed and is designed to support future JDF-based digital printing job tickets.

Xerox iGen3. Xerox (www.xerox.com) offers various digital printing solutions, including the iGen3 90/110 Digital Production Press (figure 8-8). Both models are capable of printing black-and-white and color. The iGen3 90 prints up to 90 ppm, which translates to 5,400 A4 impressions per hour. The iGen3 110 prints up to 120 ppm, or 6,600 A4 impressions per hour.

The output resolution of the iGen3 is 600×600 dpi at an 8-bit depth, which provides for continuous-tone input for ultra-sharp images and 256-level tone reproduction curves for each color separation. Halftone images are output at 150 lpi, 175 lpi, and 200 lpi, as well as stochastic,

The iGen3 can have up to six input feeder modules with two trays each, with each tray holding 2,500 120-gsm sheets for a total capacity of 30,000 sheets. Paper capacity with a roller sheeter is up to 50,000 additional sheets. The iGen3 can print on a wide variety of stocks, including coated, uncoated, textured, smooth and speciality, and mixed-stock jobs are supported at rated speeds. The paper size ranges from 7×7 in. (178×178 mm) to 14.33×20.5 in. (364×521 mm).

The iGen3 is available with a choice of high-performance RIPs: Xerox DocuSP Color Controller, EFI Fiery Color Server or Creo Spire Color Server.

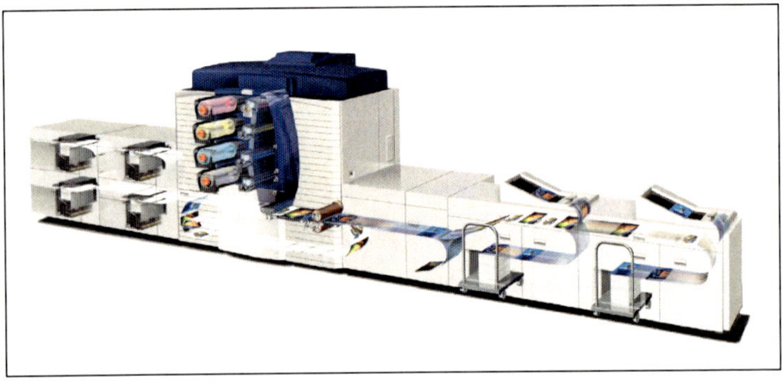

Figure 8-8. Xerox iGen3 90/110 Digital Production Press. (Courtesy Xerox Corporation)

Xerox DocuTech 6180 Production Publisher. Xerox also offers its DocuTech series of black-and-white digital presses. The Xerox DocuTech 6180 Production Publisher (figure 8-9) has an output resolution of 600×600 dpi and features high-volume production printing at speeds of 180 ppm.

Standard paper sizes range from 8×10 in. to 14.33×17 in. (203×254 mm to 364×432 mm). However, a narrow-format option is available for printing on stock only 7 in. (178 mm) wide, and an extra-large-format option is available for printing on stock up to 14.33×19.2 in. (364×488 mm). The DocuTech 180 supports a range of paper weights from 16-lb. (60-gsm) bond to 100-lb. (181-gsm) index, and a lightweight paper option allows printing of 13-lb. (49-gsm) bond. It has versatile paper input options (up to six paper trays).

The DocuTech 180 includes the DocuSP front end, which provides a common workflow across all Xerox digital production systems, to ensure the highest levels of productivity in all print environments. It also integrates with the Xerox FreeFlow™ Digital Workflow collection to help streamline operations, reduce resources, lower overhead costs, and support new applications,

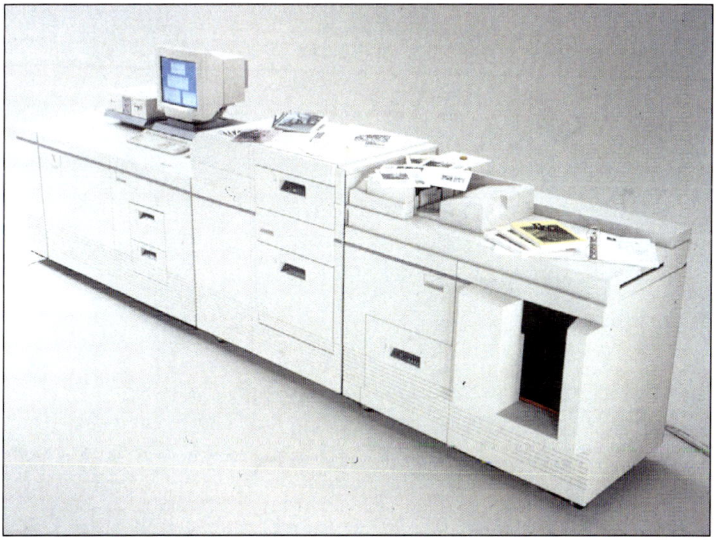

Figure 8-9. *Xerox DocuTech 6180 Production Publisher. (Courtesy Xerox Corporation)*

and it provides advanced print production features such as job ticketing programming, interposer programming, and ordered set recovery.

THERMAL WAX TRANSFER

Thermal wax transfer is a printing process that transfers a waxlike ink onto paper. In one method, a Mylar ribbon is used that contains several hundred repeating sets of full pages of black, cyan, magenta, and yellow ink. In another method, the wax is provided in solid form and then melted for transfer. The ink applied in the thermal wax transfer methods is solid at normal temperature. A sheet of paper is pressed against each color and passed by a line of heating elements that transfers the spots, or pixels, of ink onto the paper. The back of the color ribbon is in direct contact with the heated surface of the thermal head, which reaches temperatures of approximately 660°F (350°C). The image is built up of the three subtractive primary colors, cyan, magenta and yellow, with black as an optional extra. The colors are carried on the ribbon as

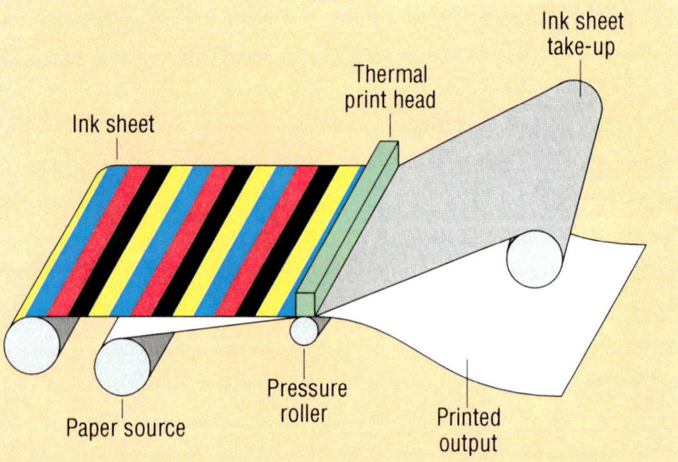

The colorant sheet has strips of cyan, magenta, yellow, and (sometimes) black, which pass under the thermal print head. The print head heats the colorant and vaporizes or melts it on to the paper.

Figure 8-10. *Principle of thermal transfer printing. (Reprinted from* Understanding Digital Color, *published by PIA/GATF* Press)

Principle of Thermal Transfer

1. Send print paper together with an ink ribbon into the space between a head and a platen roller.
2. Run electric current into the thermal head to heat it up.
3. The head and roller put pressure on the print paper and ink ribbon as they go through.
4. The heated thermal head changes the solid ink applied on the ribbon into liquid.
5. The liquid ink is transferred from the ink ribbon to the paper and absorbed by the paper.

sequential panels, and in the printing process, the ribbon moves forward continuously while the receiver is recycled underneath it, so that the whole image is written in yellow, then in magenta, and finally cyan.

The amount of ink absorbed by the paper is able to be controlled by the amount of electric current running into the thermal head. By controlling this amount, gradation reproduction by ink density is possible in this printing method. The major advantages of thermal wax printers include their relatively low cost and the high opacity of the wax, which makes them ideal for creating overhead transparencies. The disadvantages of some thermal wax printers can include speed and quality, plus the need for special paper.

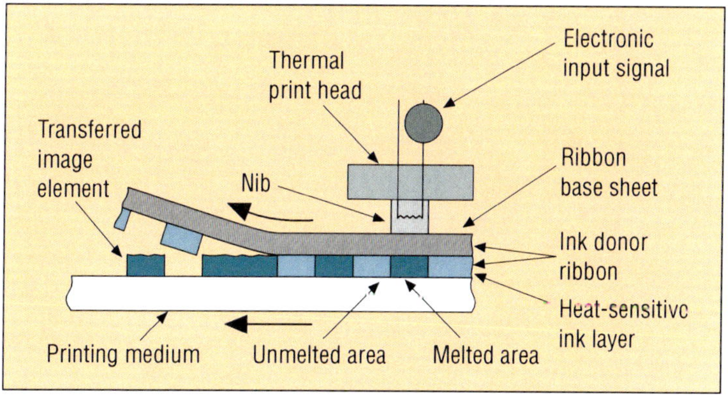

Figure 8-11. *Basic principle of thermal transfer printing. (Courtesy* Journal of Applied Photographic Engineering, *vol 7, 1981 by SPSE)*

INKJET

Inkjet is a computer-to-print technology in which digital signals drive drops of ink through a print head directly onto a substrate. Inkjet printing differs from other plateless digital technologies, like toner-based technologies, because it is primarily noncontact. Inkjet has the ability to print on a wide variety of materials, including non-flat surfaces, in addition to short-run print and variable information benefits.

Continuous inkjet (CIJ) and ***drop-on-demand (DOD)*** are different in the manner in which they propel ink to a substrate. Most addressing and document inkjet systems use CIJ technologies, where drops of ink are generated in a stream and deflected through a plate to the substrate (figure 8-12). CIJ inkjet systems have speeds to 1,000 fpm (feet per minute), which is much faster than DOD technology, but the image quality is lower than that with DOD technology.

CIJ utilizes solvent-based dyes, and the solvents are fast drying, mostly because of the use of alcohols. Viscosity requirements are low, and nozzle diameters tend to be just a few microns. With DOD, a digital signal produces a single drop of ink on the substrate rather than a stream of ink. Color is formed in a precise

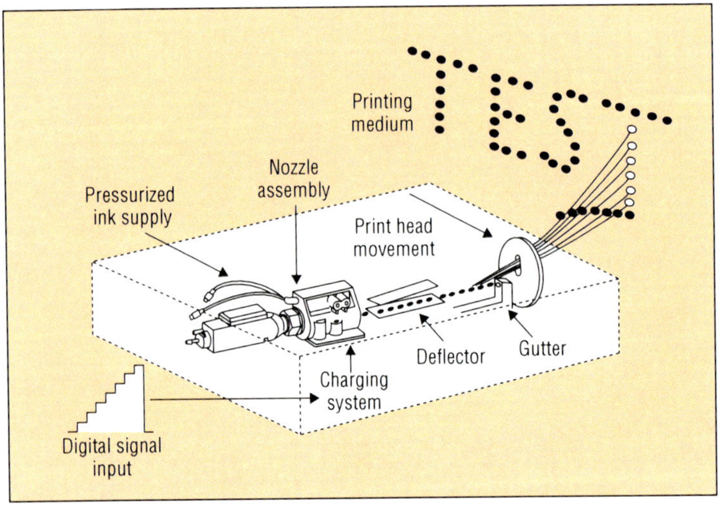

Figure 8-12. *Digital continuous inkjet. (Courtesy Marconi Data Systems, Inc.)*

arrangement of dots. Piezoelectric and thermal bubblejet drop-on-demand (DOD) inkjet printers (figures 8-13 and 8-14) dominate desktop office printing, wide format, and direct mail addressing.

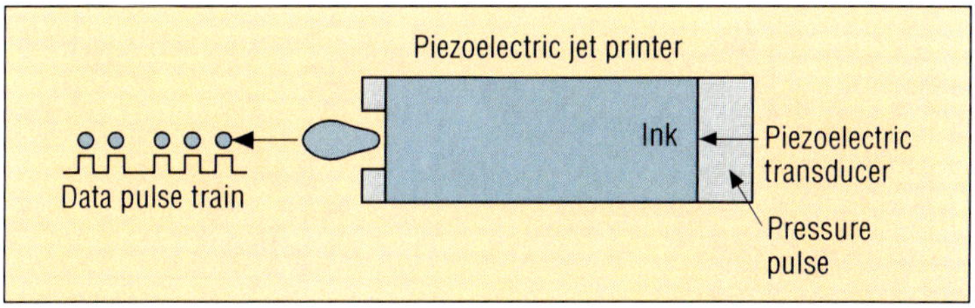

Figure 8-13. *Operating principle of piezoelectric drop-on-demand inkjet printer. (Courtesy PIRA International)*

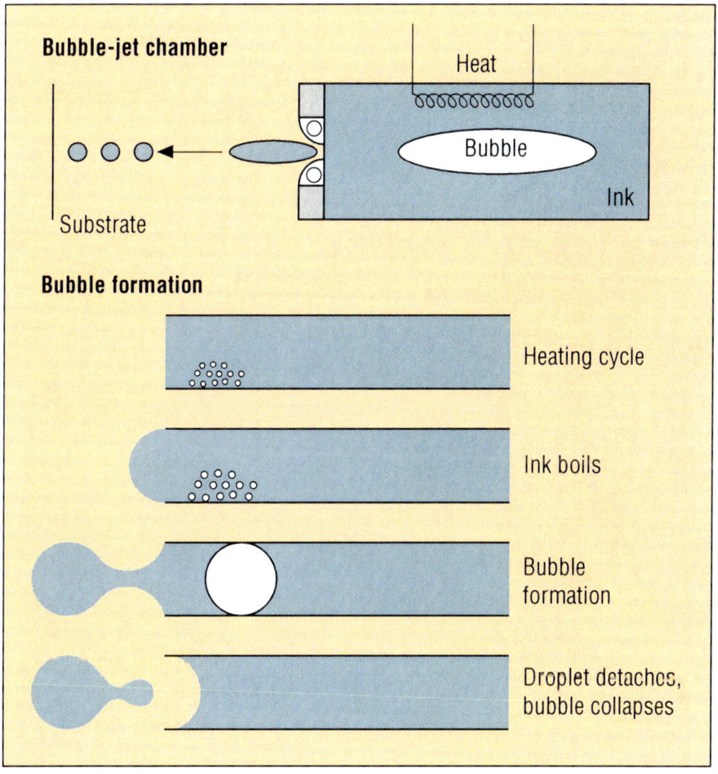

Figure 8-14. *Operating principle of thermal bubblejet drop-on-demand inkjet printer. (Courtesy PIRA International)*

Piezo DOD is also used in textile and packaging applications. Thermal DOD inkjet printers use a resistive element to create the "bubble" by generating heat, and require thermally resistive colorants. Viscosity requirements are more liberal, and the drying requirements are lower than those in CIJ. In inkjet printing today, speed and print quality are balanced because of limitations in both CIJ and DOD approaches.

DOD is the choice for full-color, high-quality printing. DOD printing can produce near-photographic quality. DOD can handle print speeds up to 300 fpm or more. Applications for DOD include packaging, point-of-purchase displays, textile, and large format/signage.

DOD versus CIJ

Continuous inkjet, as exemplified by the Kodak Versamark, will see developments in solvent-based inks that will allow packaging and converting applications. We expect a new generation of printers and inks from Versamark as Kodak exploits its inkjet research investments. For the present, DOD appears to have the edge. In the DOD space, the two leading print head developers are Spectra

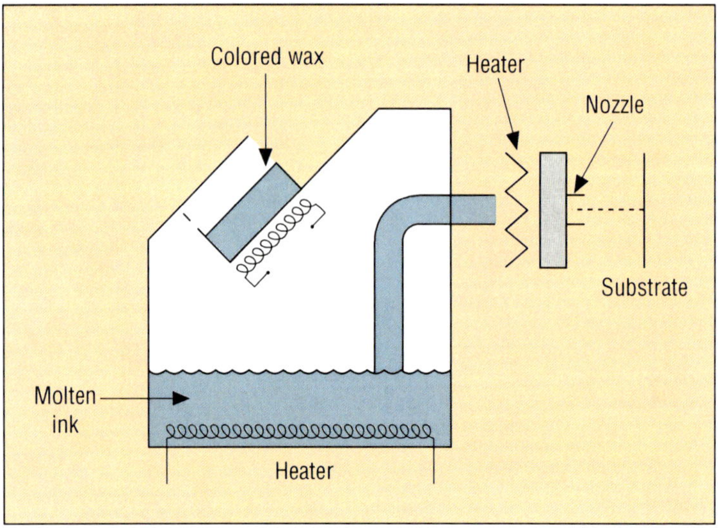

Figure 8-15. Operating principle of hot-melt drop-on-demand inkjet printer. (Courtesy PIRA International)

and Xaar. Each has a significant group of users. In 2005, 32% of the inkjet systems available were used for wide-format printing and 23% of the inkjet printers used for wide format were piezo.

Roll vs Flatbed

Most of the wide-format inkjet printers are roll-fed with a few that are flatbed. The same is true of inkjet printers used for packaging. We project that flatbed will be used for the majority of packaging printing and roll-fed for document and variable-data printing. By 2010, 67% of all packaging graphics printed with inkjet will be printed on flatbed printers. Inkjet quality and speed are increasing daily.

9. Toners and Inks for Digital Printing

TONER BASICS

Toner is a complex powder that an electrophotographic engine uses to form an image. Laser printers and copiers form the image as charges of electricity, attract toner particles to those charges, and then melt the toner onto the paper. What started off as a powder becomes a fluid and ends up as a solid.

Think of toner as a very small capsule with a pigment inside that can hold an electrical charge.

Toner is a blend of plastic resins, coloring pigments/dyes, waxes, flow agents, charge agents, and other ingredients needed to make those resins and colors to create a toner with proper charging, transferring, and fusing characteristics. The resins give toner its overall physical ability to be first a fine powder, next melt at a relatively low temperature, and then form a permanent plastic solid capable of bonding with paper fibers. In the case of magnetic toner, the main ingredient is normally magnetic iron oxide.

Major Categories of Toner

There are three major groups of toners

- Dual component
- Mono component
- Liquid

Dual-component toner. Dual-component toner, which is used in over 90% of the current xerographic copiers and digital printers, is made up of toner and carrier beads. Cascade development is the most common method used with a dual-component toner. In cascade development, the toner mixture is poured or "cascaded" over the inclined surface bearing an electrostatic latent image.

Carrier beads are about 70 to 400 microns in diameter (a micron being one thousandth of a millimeter) and usually consist of a metallic or magnetic compound. Carrier beads are made up

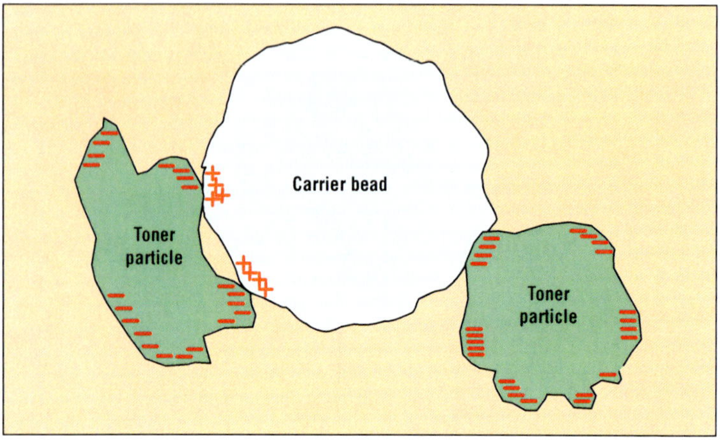

Figure 9-1. The function of carrier beads in transporting the toner particles.

of a blend of organically treated inorganic fine powder which acts as a developer and lubricant, while providing releasability. Because the toner particles are insulative, toner images on the photoreceptor are easily transferred electrostatically to plain paper. These particles are small, charged pigment particles and attach themselves to much larger carrier beads (figure 9-1). A single carrier bead can hold multiple toner particles. The name "carrier bead" comes from the idea of "carrying" the fine toner particles to the latent electrostatic image where the toner is stripped from the carrier, thereby developing the image.

Carrier beads are magnetic materials that are specially coated with a polymeric film to provide the proper triboelectric properties for attracting toner. The magnetic material can then be transported from one location to another through the use of magnetic fields. Methods are used to adhere dual-component toner particles to a charged material until it is torn away from that material, primarily by the competing electrostatic force exerted by the electrostatic latent image.

Mono-component toner. Mono-component toner is the all-in-one type. Mono-component toner differs from dual-component toner in that it does not require the use of carrier beads for development. Instead, it contains the pigments for printing as well as its own carrier to transport the toner from hopper to paper.

The magnetic type of mono-component toner has iron oxide encapsulated within each individual toner particle making it possible for the magnetic roller to pick it up and hold it. This is the type of toner in Canon and other printer engines. All mono-component systems that use magnetic developer rollers must have magnetic toner.

The second type of mono-component toner is the non-magnetic type. In this case, a static charge created through friction is sufficient to pick up and hold the toner on the surface of the roller. In some cases, the developer rollers are a rubber compound to which the non-magnetic toner is naturally attracted.

There are several ways to charge mono-component toners—induction, contacting, corona charging, ion beam, and traveling electric fields. The easiest and most commonly used of these is induction charging. Through induction charging, a conducting particle sitting on a negative surface becomes negatively charged.

Liquid toner. Liquid toner consists of a toner and a solvent. The use of solvent instead of carrier beads (developer) causes them to be liquid instead of solid. Liquid toner solvents are non-conductive and primarily made up of thermoplastic resin particles, which are suspended in a saturated hydrocarbon. In many respects liquid development is related to or considered with powder-cloud development. In both cases, freely moving charged toner moves under the action of the electrostatic field of the image. Currently Indigo is the only major user of liquid toner. Indigo's liquid toner consists of toner particles suspended in a highly refined kerosene known as isopar. The isopar acts as the controlling agent of the solution by carrying the charge placed on it. (See sidebar on next page.)

Tribolectric Properties of Toner—"Toner Chargeability"

A ***triboelectric charge*** is a friction-induced static charge between two dissimilar materials. The electrical charge on laser printer toners is derived from triboelectric (static electricity) properties. When toner is rubbed across a developer roller it builds up a static charge similar to running a comb through dry hair, or even petting your long-haired cat during the winter. This causes excited

HP/INDIGO ELECTROINK

Unlike other electrophotography-based digital presses that use dry toner, the HP/Indigo uses a special patented liquid ink, called ***ElectroInk,*** which uses pigments similar to those in regular offset inks but with two dramatic differences: (1) it acts electrostatically, meaning it can be charged, and (2) it dries very quickly. Contained in the toners is a dispersion of pigmented polymer particles ranging in size from 1 to 2 microns. In contrast, the dry toner particles used in copy machines have an average size of 8–15 microns. When transferred to the blanket and heated, these polymers turn into a tacky polymeric "film."

When the ink film polymer comes in contact with the substrate, it hardens instantly and peels away from the blanket. There are two interesting contrasts with traditional printing. First, the toner does not bind with the substrate paper as in traditional printing but laminates or coats the substrate. Second, 100% of the toner is removed with each revolution, while in the conventional offset printing process, half of the ink is transferred to the paper and the balance stays on the blanket, to be re-inked on the next revolution.

toner particles to cling to a beaded carrier. Triboelectric characteristics of toner will influence image quality as well as yield.

Once toner particles become charged they can be transferred to the substrate. This change in charge causes toner to move in an opposite direction of a magnetic roller forming a conductive path. It is then attracted to the latent image and adhered to the substrate by a photoreceptor and Coulomb force. The toner must have stable triboelectrical characteristics for extended time periods for dispersion of the resin and wax.

The chargeability of individual toners is related to the particle size. Smaller-than-average particles tend to charge to a higher value within a given charge time. In addition, toner particles will charge uniformly when they are of the same average size and composition.

The magnitude and polarity of toner charge is critical. The charge on the toner must have the correct polarity or no development will occur. The magnitude of the charge is also critical because the development force is directly proportional to toner charge. Development will occur only when the electrostatic development force exceeds the adhesive force.

In many cases, the carrier beads are coated with a polymer that transfers the amount of charge to the toner. Carrier coatings and toner materials can be selected from a tribo series, which is a listing of polymers in order of charging polarity. The tribo series lists polymers according to charge; polymers appearing higher on the list will charge positively with respect to any polymer lower on the list. The total amount of charge exchange between the toner and the carrier is a function of the total number of toner particles contained on each carrier bead.

The concept that relates the chargeability of a mass of toner is measured by Q divided by M, or charge divided by the mass that was transferred. This measurement is used for process control, as is particle distribution. The ability of a laser cartridge to maintain the same Q/M ratio within its supply is dependent on the quality of the toner and the efficiency of the development system.

Toner Size and Its Relationship to Resolution

Toner is 1 to 30 microns in size, depending on the desired resolution of the printed image. The higher the resolution, the smaller the toner particles needed to output that resolution. When laser printers first entered the market in the 1980s, toner particles were an average of 12 microns in diameter, about half the width of a human hair, and corresponded to the laser beam diameter of 300-dpi printers. Within two years, the average toner particle size was down to about 8 microns—sometimes called ***microfine toner.*** The 8-micron toner coincided with the emergence of 600-dpi print resolution.

Toner Concentration

The image density is highly dependent on the concentration of toner within a given area. Image density is not completely determined by charge because environmental conditions such as humidity and temperature also have an effect. Toner concentration may vary from 0.5% to approximately 2% by weight, depending upon a number of chemical and reproduction variables.

Toner Transfer Efficiency

The toner transfer efficiency of printers and copiers is 85%. The 15% scraped off the organic photoconductor (OPC) drum or belt is waste. In the U.S., around 21 million pounds of waste toner is disposed of annually. It is non-toxic and inert, so it is deposited into landfills. Less than 1% of U.S. waste toner is recycled.

The toners that are available for transfer to the OPC are a cross-section of the entire distribution. It is reasonable to expect that all particles within the size spectrum will be developed. It is that mass of toner that is offered to the OPC drum or belt that will develop.

TONER MANUFACTURE

The majority of toners are still manufactured using a mechanical melt mixing or hot compounding process. The resins, carbon black, magnetic iron oxides, waxes, and charge control agents are blended while molten to form a hot paste. This viscous mixture is then cooled either by slabbing it out, by extruding it onto a cooling belt, or by pelletizing it and cooling the pellets. This raw toner is then ground to a powder by jet mills or air-swept hammer mills. These processes produce a wide variety of particle sizes. The oversize and undersize toner particles are sifted out in a multi-pass process.

The pulverized, sifted toner powder is then blended with additives to adjust flow and electrostatic properties. This final blending is critical and hard to control, especially when the additive particle size is different from the toner particle size. For toner produced this way, an average toner particle of about 8 microns is about as small as you can get.

Chemically made toner particles are round or "potato" shaped, not jagged like pulverized toner (figure 9-2). Smooth particles flow better in the powder state and hold a more uniform electrostatic charge in the laser printer. They are also 4 microns in diameter. You need 40% less 4-micron toner than 8-micron toner to print the same thing.

The Xerox EA Technology process uses a controlled method to chemically grow toner particles from molecules up to particles of any desired size and shape. Conventional toner is created by pulverizing chunks of toner compound and sifting them to collect the proper size of toner particles. While conventional methods have been improved over time to maximize toner yields and performance, the mechanical methods were still energy-intensive. The EA Technology process is far more environmentally friendly,

Figure 9-2. Photomicrograph of pulverized toner particles (left) and chemical toner particles (right). (Courtesy Xerox Corporation)

using much less energy since the toner particles are produced by non-mechanical means. It is a water-based, low-energy process in which particles are "grown" to the required size. They are isolated from the growth compound and processed for use.

The quality of the printing with toners from EA Technology is approaching that of offset printing with liquid ink because of the extremely small size of the toner particles, often measuring between 4 and 5 microns, about half the size of previous toner particles. Because of the new material's size and uniform circular shape, the toner particles transfer efficiently and uniformly to the receiving paper, wasting less and needing less to form the print. This results in color prints that more accurately depict subtle, graded or shifting tones and hues or complex, intricate patterns.

QUALITY CONSIDERATIONS WITH TONERS

The quality and dependability of the toner starts with the quality of the components, which must then be thoroughly mixed to precise ratios. Every characteristic of the toner is critical to its effectiveness.

Any inconsistency in the mixture will create problems. The toner mixture must also be ground down to a narrow range of very small and specific particle sizes. Since it is not possible at present to have a uniform particle size, there always will be variation in the image quality over the printing life of some cartridges. ***Backgrounding*** from improperly charged or wrong-signed particles can also be an issue. Backgrounding is the most commonly observed issue with image performance.

Charge Properties of Toner

Charge properties are crucial to proper transfer of the toner. Improper charge properties of the toner can lead to backgrounding, blasting, or light print. The toner's charging characteristics depend on the particle size, shape, and composition of the toner. A triboelectric charge is generated on the toner particles through friction. The charge generated on each particle is dependent on the surface area to mass ratio of the particle. This ratio is determined by the size and shape of the particles. A smaller particle has a larger surface area to mass ratio than does a larger particle. This produces a stronger triboelectric charge on the smaller particles. This is significant since particles of varying charges will move at different rates, which results in particle sorting and can cause print defects.

It is very important to have the particles as uniformly sized as possible. This requires several siftings of the toner after it has been ground to a fine powder. Charge agents are equally as important in determining how well the particles charge and even if the toner will charge negatively or positively.

Fusing Ability of Toner

Toner fusing ability requires specific melting and adhering properties. It must melt at the proper temperature to be compatible with the fusing system it will be used in. Not only is the melting point important, but the fusing rate is also very important. Toners for higher-speed printers must respond to the challenge to fuse more quickly than toners for lower-speed printers. Toners that do not meet these requirements can cause ***cold offset*** or ***hot offset,*** which is a ghost image picked up in the fuser. The fusing properties of the toner are determined by the plastic resins used as well as additives.

Yet another consideration that must be taken into account is the flow rate of the toner. The flow rate of the toner can significantly affect the density of the print. A better flowing toner will produce higher-density prints. An optimum flow rate must be achieved. Clearly the toner must not be too fluid or that will present problems of its own, while a toner that is not fluid enough will also create problems. Flow rate is determined by composition, particle size, and additives.

Print Quality Considerations

The toner must charge, transfer, and fuse properly to produce a good image. Even if these factors are working together well, there still may be print quality issues.

Take for instance image resolution. If the printer is capable of 1200-dpi resolution, the toner should be also. This requires a microfine toner, with very small particle size, usually six microns or less. A toner with larger particle sizes may work very well in the printer if it meets all of the other requirements. That is, it will transfer and fuse to the paper nicely and produce dark prints with no blasting or backgrounding, but it will not produce the razor sharp images the end user may be looking for with their high-resolution printer.

Not only will particle size affect the resolution of the print but it will also affect the density and even limit the variety of shades a printer is able to produce. Shades are produced by printing black dots in white areas. The blackness of the dots is always the same, they appear to be darker or lighter, however, depending on how many there are per any given area or, in other words, how closely grouped they are. Suppose a printer places one hundred dots per square inch to create a certain level of shading. If the particle size of the toner is too large to stay within the boundaries of the intended dot size, the toner will fill in more of the area than intended and a darker shade will be produced. This is how toners with larger particle sizes limit the shading spectrum of printers with high-resolution capabilities.

Not only must all these factors work together perfectly, but they need to do so under adverse conditions. Operating environment can and does affect a toner's ability to perform properly. Even the best toners can sometimes be affected by extreme temperatures and/or humidity.

INKJET INK

Inks for printing systems include water-, oil- and solvent-based inks and energy-curable inks. Advancements in inkjet inks provide the flexibility to print on just about any medium. The digital device will be used to print variable data—graphics or text required to change during the run.

Digital UV Inks

The digital printing market is undergoing an ultraviolet (UV) revolution. UV inkjet technology has been around for many years in the cable and wire industry, but the application has been limited due to ink viscosity restrictions inherent with continuous inkjet printheads. During the past five years, new printheads based on piezo technology has been developed, and the result has been a dramatic increase in the range of ink viscosity. Digital inks are over 50 times thinner than their nearest screen printing equivalent.

One of the advantages of UV ink is the instant dry feature that leaves the image completely cured so that no solvents penetrate the substrate once it is printed. Instant drying requires less substrate dependence. Since UV inks don't dry on the printhead, some of the problems associated with cleaning and purging the head to remove insoluble material are avoided. Theoretically, greater print production rates are achievable with UV ink because you don't have to wait for drying solvents or perform constant maintenance.

UV-curing inks change from a liquid to a solid state when polymerization takes place under exposure to ultraviolet (UV) light. This UV light initiates a chemical reaction, which generates a matrix of cross-linked materials to give the solid ink film chemical resistance, gloss, and scratch resistance. The ink has a low molecular weight and low viscosity, but the polymerization reaction initiated by UV exposure generates a high-impact solid, resulting in a cured ink film. UV ink systems have a three-decade record in the screen printing market where a typical mesh hole of 30 microns is used.

UV inks have pigment particles of less than a micron, which are evenly dispersed within the carrier and retain that dispersion. An inkjet nozzle on the Inca Eagle, for example, has an opening similar to the diameter of a human hair, so one oversize pigment particle could be a problem. The correct ratio and type of monomers (reactive diluents), oligomers (reactive resins), and photoinitiators (UV light absorbers) capable of producing stable low-viscosity ink suitable for inkjetting effectively are essential. Sericol has optimized the surface tension, viscosity, and overall physical properties of the ink to control both print quality and adhesion performance. This means that digital UV ink can apply to the widest range of substrates possible. Because UV-curable inks are nonvolatile, the life of the printhead increases.

UV inks result in consistent images from substrate to substrate. And there are environmental advantages over solvent inks as UV boasts fewer emissions. The ideal UV-curable inkjet inks will enable printed images to have water resistance, fade resistance, no volatile organic compounds (VOCs), and media flexibility. The requirement for lamination will also diminish as UV inks are used. There are three approaches to UV inks—water-based, hot-melt, and low-viscosity versions.

Water-based UV ink. Water-based UV inkjet technology is attracting attention because it uses water to produce lower viscosity. Water-based UV inks are formulated with UV-curable resin emulsions. However, to function efficiently, the system needs to eliminate the water before the UV lamp cures the ink. Eliminating the water is difficult as you want to cure as quickly as possible to prevent undesirable dot gain, wicking, or feathering into the substrate. If water is present, the ink will not adhere to the substrate. UV curable inks that are 100% solids will be the first product available.

Hot-melt inkjet ink. Hot-melt inkjet inks are dependent upon a large viscosity drop that could occur with specialty inkjet formulations. There may or may not be wear and abrasion or cracking with flexible substrates.

Low-viscosity UV inks. There are also UV inks based on low-viscosity versions of conventional UV formulations. The low-viscosity UV curable inks are designed to work with piezo printheads. The higher-viscosity inks are for use with industrial printheads such as the Spectra or Xaar products. The ink is available in process colors (standard and light shades) and a custom spot color.

Cost comparisons of UV inks and conventional inks. UV-curable inks are more costly than conventional inks due to the specialty raw materials used in the formulations. UV inks can be up to two to three times the cost of conventional inks.

Environmental considerations with UV inks. Some UV raw materials can result in irritation and sensitization, and some UV lamp systems generate ozone that must be vented or neutralized. Inkjet printers generate a very small amount of mist that must be removed from the printer enclosure.

Collaboration among vendors. Collaboration among vendors is a key to success. inkjet ink manufacturers must work closely with UV lamp and chemical companies. Spectra, for example, collaborates with American Inkjet, Flint Ink, Durst, Inkware, Vutek, Inca, and Sericol.

Pigments

Pigments have substantially superior lightfast properties and chemical resistance than dyes. However, their insolubility and particle size make them a challenge to use in inkjet printing. While the use of carbon black and titanium dioxide is commonplace, use of other pigments has been limited. Whereas dyes are soluble, pigments are insoluble and must be dispersed. This creates the need to reduce the pigment particle to a size that is submicron, and the need to stabilize the dispersion and limit re-agglomeration. Pigment particles need to be less than 1 micron for drop-on-demand (DOD) applications and less than 0.5 microns for continuous inkjet (CIJ). One approach to making pigments stable is to modify their chemical makeup. Pigments provide more saturated color and will dominate in inkjet printing.

10. Data Acquisition, Management, and Enrichment

WHAT IS A DATABASE AND HOW DID THEY DEVELOP?

A ***database*** is an organized collection of data. Databases have been around for decades. The first known use of the word "data base" was in 1963 at a symposium entitled "Development and Management of a Computer-Centered Data Base" and sponsored by the System Development Corporation. Although "data base" was two words at this point, by the late 1970s the single word, "database," was used regularly to describe an organized collection of data. Prior to the digital era, databases were created on a typewriter. Lists were created that were, in fact, the database. The lists could also be typed onto paper labels for direct mail pieces. Technology improved with the development of address label printers, such as the Cheshire 730 model, that could print labels by photoscanning data onto labels. It was the development of the PC computer in the early 1980s that really enabled databases to develop into what we know of them today. Once storage media became available to store the data, a tremendous growth in database creation, management, and manipulation began to occur. Finally for the first time data could be stored, retrieved, and manipulated. As the cost of PCs and storage devices started to decrease, it really accelerated the availability and timeliness of databases because now more people could input and access data.

Today, the data is used in a computer system in the form of a data file and can be readily accessed and sorted. Most database files consist of fields and records. An example of a field would be a person's first name or their last name. Some very simple fields for VDP would include first name, last name, street address, city, state, and zip code. Each of these fields for one individual would combine together to make a record. An example of a record would be as follows:

Jane Smith
1 Grand Avenue
San Luis Obispo, CA 93407

DATABASE MODELS AND STRUCTURES

A database, then, can also be a collection of records or facts held within the file. The structural description of these facts is known as the ***schema.*** The schema describes the facts that are represented in the database and the relationship between them. The method in which the schema is organized is known as the database model or how the database structure is modeled. The two main database models are the flat model and the relational model.

A ***flat model*** is a single, two-dimensional array of data elements usually containing rows and columns, as shown in figure 10-1 below.

◇	A	B
1	**First**	**Last**
2	Harvey	Levenson
3	Mike	Blum
4	Malcolm	Keif
5	Penny	Bennett
6	Lorraine	Donegan
7	Xiaoying	Rong
8	Kevin	Cooper
9	Ken	Macro
10	Hal	Hinderliter
11	Brian	Lawler

Figure 10-1. *An example of a flat model database.*

Using this model, the data in a given column are assumed to have a similar value, in this case column A is all first names. In each row the data is assumed to be associated with one another. For example, row 2 has one individual's first and last name in the row. This model is the basis of a spreadsheet and, in fact, Microsoft Excel can be used to create and manipulate data for VDP projects. A flat model, sometimes referred to as a flat file, is used for small amounts of data and works well with data that can be edited in a less automated environment. Although Microsoft Excel is commonly used for data processing needs, there are several reasons why a flat file in Excel could be problematic. Excel has a limitation on the number of records and fields that may be used: a maximum of 256 fields and 65,536 records. Sorting in Excel is much slower than in database software, mainly because databases index fields for quick sorts. Excel files can easily sort; but if not done carefully, this sorting can quickly scramble the data between records. This type of error is not a problem with database software. Sorting and filtering of large amounts of data in a flat model can be time-consuming and require a great deal of computing power. This is because the computer has to go through each data item to search and sort. It is not an efficient method for large amounts of data. Elements within a flat file are usually separated using a common delimiter such as a comma, space, or tab. Sorting and filtering then requires the computer to go through each delimiter to find the related data.

A ***relational model*** contains multiple tables similar to the one table created by the flat file. The tables can then relate to each other and be linked through a key field. This makes the sorting and filtering much more efficient. For example, one file can contain multiple tables where one table is an "Authors" table and the other table is a "Books" table, as shown in figure 10-2. In this example, a relationship can be determined between the two to

	A	B	C	
1	**First**	**Last**	**Author ID**	
2	Harvey	Levenson	HL1	
3	Mike	Blum	MB1	
4	Malcolm	Keif	MK1	
5	Penny	Bennett	PB1	
6	Lorraine	Donegan	LD1	
7	Xiaoying	Rong	XR1	
8	Kevin	Cooper	KC1	
9	Ken	Macro	KM1	
10	Hal	Hinderliter	HH1	
11	Brian	Lawler	BL1	

1	**Title**	**Author ID**
2	Introduction to Graphic Communication	HL1
3	Desktop Publishing Primer	HH1
4	Official Adobe Print Publishing Guide	BL1

Figure 10-2. *An example of a relational database model consisting of two tables—an "Authors" table (top) and a "Books" table (bottom).*

find out more information about a particular author. A key field of "Author ID" would exist in each table to link the two together.

The structure within a relational model is much more efficient than in a flat model. In the 1970s, E.F. Codd devised rules of data normalization that make a relational model much more efficient than a flat model. Common examples of database programs that uses a relational model are Microsoft Access and FileMaker Pro. Other, more robust database systems, such as Microsoft SQL and Oracle, use the relational model as well. These will be discussed in more detail later.

DATABASE FILE FORMATS

Once a database is created, it can be saved in a variety of database formats. Some common database file formats followed by their three-digit file extension are shown in table 10-1.

Table 10-1. Common Database Formats

Comma delimited (known as ***comma-separated values***)	.csv
Tab delimited	.txt
Microsoft Excel	.xls
Microsoft Access	.mdb
FileMaker Pro	.fp7
dBase format	.dbf
Data interchange format	.dif
SYLK	.slk

Some simpler formats such as tab-delimited (.txt) or comma-separated values (.csv) would be used for flat model database formats. These two formats are actually text formats, making them very simple and consequently a smaller file size than other formats. One advantage of these simpler formats is they are very compatible and can be good formats to transfer files between programs and computers. Because of the basic nature inherent in a text file, these can also be good formats for retrieving and exchanging data from older legacy systems for things such as customer databases. The data can them be transferred and manipulated into formats more conducive to today's data requirements.

Text formats can save the field names as well as the data, but these formats generally don't save the data type stored in the field (e.g., text, number, date, etc.). DBF is popular because it saves all of the header information.

Microsoft Excel, FileMaker Pro, and Microsoft Access are considered ***native formats*** because they are formats created by the original, native application. This does not mean that these formats are not compatible with other systems, however. There are many VDP software programs that will allow for Excel documents to be imported directly into the program's database component. Since Microsoft Access creates relational databases, the .mdb format imports easily into database servers such as Microsoft SQL, DB2, and Oracle.

Database interchange format (.dif) and SYLK (.slk) are formats primarily used for spreadsheets and exchange of spreadsheet data. They are not designed specifically for database use but can be useful in exchanging data from spreadsheet applications.

Database format (.dbf) and Microsoft Access database (.mdb) are actually very good formats to use in VDP, especially with large amounts of data. They can contain multiple tables conducive to a relational model, which in turn, enables the format to be used with high-end database servers. These formats can store the actual data as with a flat file, but they can also store both field names and field types such as number, date, text, etc.

DATABASE FIELD TYPES

Databases can have ***fixed-length fields*** or ***variable-length fields***. With personalized printing, this needs to be taken into consideration. Anyone with a long name has seen the consequences of a fixed-length field if the last part of their name has been cut off in a mailing to them. Fixed-length fields have their advantages. They can provide an efficient means of storing and searching records. But this type of database requires careful planning to anticipate the longest field that may be encountered. Aesthetically, it is not a good idea to cut off or abbreviate data within a field, so this should be avoided.

Most database software provides the option to save each field to hold a specific type of data, e.g., data, text, number, etc. Some applications provide fine distinctions such as floating point numbers versus integers. Careful planning is again required in the proper choice of field type, and a poor decision can return to haunt you. For example, it might appear obvious that a zip code should be stored as a number. However, storing a zip code such as 02135 (Brighton, MA) as a number, would cause it to change to a proper numeric format 2135, which is an incorrect zip code. Therefore zip codes are typically stored as text fields.

DATABASE SERVERS

A ***database server*** is a computer that uses a specialized process to manage the database itself. Most database servers work with relational databases. Database servers are based on a client/server architecture. This helps lower the network traffic with large databases by allowing a client to connect to the server and only access the files needed. A query can be done on the database to determine what files are needed based on certain search parameters. This is usually done using the ***Structured Query Language (SQL),*** which is a language used by most database servers today. Some commercial available database servers are:

- mSQL
- MySQL
- Oracle
- DB2
- Microsoft SQL Server

DATABASES AND VDP

So what does all this mean and how is it used in VDP? Generally speaking, it will depend on the amount of data and the number of records being incorporated into a VDP project. Jobs requiring smaller or even moderate amounts of data may not require the use of a database server. Much of the data can be managed and manipulated using a combination of database software programs and VDP software programs. At this level of database management, care must be taken to maintain an original database file whether it be in FileMaker Pro or Microsoft Access or Excel. If changes are made or updates are done, these must be done in the original database and then it can be re-imported into the VDP application. This will ensure a more accurate database record for your customers.

It should also be determined in the early planning stages who will be responsible for maintaining and updating the original database. It may be the customer, it may be a specialized data management agency, it may be someone within the marketing agency, or it may be the printer.

ACQUIRING, MANAGING, AND ENRICHING THE DATA

To be successful producing VDP, data is a critical component. Some say it is the MOST important component. The more data you have and the more accurate the data is, the more successful the VDP campaign will be. Have you ever gotten something in the mail that had your name spelled wrong or used your full name rather than your nickname? How personalized does that make you feel? Accurate data also means the piece is more likely to get to its destination. If the address isn't current, or if it isn't formatted according to postal regulations, it may not arrive at its destination.

Data can be acquired through a variety of sources. Sometimes the VDP customer will have a list of their own customers that they will want to use. This is a good source of data because you already know the customer will be interested in the "product" as they are already a current customer or have been a customer in the past. Another option is to purchase or rent lists from data brokers. Some caution must be used with this method because not all data brokers are reputable and the data may not be accurate. There are advantages and disadvantages to purchasing and renting lists. If you rent a list, you can only use it for the number of times it was rented for, but you don't need to worry about keeping the lists updated. Most large data solutions companies that provide lists to rent also have a very sophisticated system for collecting, managing, and updating their lists. Sometimes, this can be worth the cost to rent as opposed to buy. Two companies specializing in offering a comprehensive data solution to its customers are Accu-Data America, headquartered in Fort Myers, Florida, and USA-Data, Inc. headquartered in New York, New York.

Data can also be acquired through websites. If a personalized campaign includes a VDP mailer, the original list can be rented for sending out the mailer. If some of those people on the list then go to a website that is part of the personalized campaign and enter their information into the website, the data is now owned by the website creator. A smaller database can then be created from those accessing the website for further use in the marketing campaign. Once the data is acquired there are certain techniques that can be used to improve the overall quality of the data.

Several processes are used to improve the quality of the data in a data file, including the following processes:

- Cleansing
- Parsing
- Mining
- Modeling
- Merge/purge

Cleansing is the process of removing duplicate information, bad records, incomplete records, or errant characters. This can be done manually or automatically with some type of cleansing software or simple scripts that can be incorporated into the database (e.g., Scriptmaker in FileMaker Pro). ***Parsing*** simply means to separate or take apart. In database enrichment, it is the process of looking at parts of the file to make sure things like the field names are correct and the data has delimiters in place and is in the correct fields. ***Mining*** is the process of analyzing the data attributes to look for trends or anomalies for possible extraction. For example, extracting a list of people who are homeowners or who have children from a data file will help in developing a more targeted variable piece to them. ***Modeling*** is the process of using the data attributes to build profiles of potential buyers. Finally ***merge/purge*** is a form of cleansing that is usually done by specialized software. The software analyzes certain parts of two records; for example the first few letters of a person's first and last name, combined with a few characters from the record's address field and zip code. If enough similarities are found, then the software determines the two records are duplicates and eliminates one of the records, hence the term merge and purge.

One more step used in the process of managing and enriching data is the use of various types of address verifying or updating methods. Coding Accuracy Support System (CASS) software improves the accuracy of postal carrier routes. For example, it will verify the accuracy of both five-digit zip codes and ZIP+4 codes.

Presort Accuracy, Validation, and Evaluation (PAVE) software determines the best presorting methods to use for the most cost-effective postal rates. For keeping addresses current, there is the National Change of Address (NCOA) database that can be accessed for automatic updates of addresses when people move and fill out the change of address form through the U.S. Postal Service.

11. Cross-Media Personalized Marketing

MARKETING TRENDS

Marketing has evolved over time and has shifted from mass marketing to segmented marketing to personalized marketing. ***Mass marketing*** is marketing to a higher quantity of people but sending the same general message. Examples of mass marketing are TV, radio and newspaper marketing. ***Segmented marketing*** is a way of identifying a smaller group of people and sending a more specific message to the group based on what is known about them. For example, people who watch the Discovery Channel are identified as being mostly upscale, educated adults aged 25 to 54. Marketing towards this group can be more targeted based on what is known about the audience. ***Personalized marketing*** is sending a specific message to a specific person. It is sometimes called ***one-to-one marketing*** and ***customized marketing.*** The more that is known about someone, the more targeted the message is that can be sent. Marketers are putting a lot of effort into developing individual profiles on people to help send a more targeted message to them. This is done by gathering data through a variety of sources such as census data, mailing lists, credit card purchases, hospital records, phone bills, coupon returns, and surveys. This is sometimes called ***data mining*** and the data is then used to determine individual profiles.

Marketers won't be looking at every individual in which to build a profile. It is important to first determine who are the most likely candidates for personalized marketing. With most businesses, 80% of the company's business comes from 20% of its customers. In the airline industry, for example, the customers that are the frequent fliers generate the most profit for the airlines. Most airlines will have special programs set up to offer incentives and perks to those frequent fliers to keep their business. So it is identifying those 20% of the customers that may be the important part. If you are targeting new customers, then the factors become identifying someone with a potential interest in your product, but also identifying their income and spending habits. The best customers are going to be not only those that have money but also those who have a history of spending money, hopefully on your product.

Once some information is gathered in the form of data, it then becomes important to determine what type of message to send and how to send it. Today, there are many options for getting information to people such as TV, radio, print, email, and the Internet.

CROSS-MEDIA OPTIONS

Marketer's are realizing that mass media marketing is not always the best way to market to people. With the numbers of people having Internet access and email, marketers are developing cross-media personalized marketing campaigns that includes VDP as one component of an entire campaign.

Relevancy in communication is inherent in building relationships. If you talk to someone you don't know and you find out something you have in common, you've just established a relationship with that person. The more you find of common interest, the stronger the relationship becomes. The same concept can be applied to personalized marketing. If you know whether someone is male or female, if they are retired, or if they are homeowners, you can send a more relevant message to them.

Cross-media marketing can combine a variety of media including mass marketing, personalized marketing, or both. A cross-media personalized marketing campaign can typically include personalized email, variable-data printing (figure 11-1), and a personalized URL (figure 11-2).

Personalized emails are the most cost-effective part of a campaign. The only information needed is a person's first name and email address. Just as with VDP, the more information you have for a person, the more relevant the message can become. All that is needed to send personalized emails are a database and a web server. The potential disadvantages of personalized emails include the use of email filters and the danger of marketing fatigue by consumers. Most email clients and email servers have SPAM filters available for activation that can essentially block all messages from going to that address. Many email users are becoming

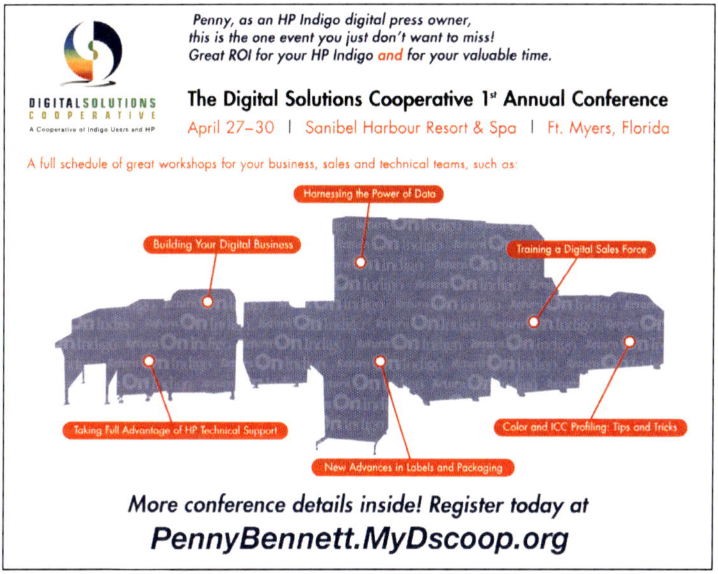

Figure 11-1. A VDP marketing piece that included a personalized URL.

Figure 11-2. After entering the personalized URL shown in figure 11-1, the recipient of the VDP marketing piece is taken to this personalized web page.

frustrated with email marketing messages. Potential legislation could be passed one day that prevents marketing to email accounts. More likely, however, will be a "do not email" list implemented by the government similar to the "do not call" list implemented in 2003 preventing telephone marketing to those on the list. If this happens, VDP will become even more popular as a means of marketing.

When designing the personalized emails, it is important to remember they should always include hyperlinks for the user to click on that will direct them to a landing page or personalized URL. It is also important to have more than one opportunity for the user to click on the link. There should be at least two if not more links available. The emails should be designed in HTML rather than plain text. This provides for much more creativity and allows a much better design to be sent to the customer. Remember, if you get through the SPAM filter, you likely only have a fraction of a second to get the customer's attention before the delete key is activated.

An extremely important part of the personalized marketing campaign is the creation of a web page to direct the consumer to. Ideally, a personalized URL would have more impact than a static web page. If data exists on a given individual, then the web page should be populated with that information. The more convenient it is for a person to take action, the more likely they are to do so. Once a consumer goes to a web page, they then become a user that has opted in to the marketing campaign. More data can then be gathered to create and send more relevant marketing messages to the consumer.

Where does VDP fit into a personalized marketing campaign? A personalized printed piece can be sent to the consumer initially in the form of a business reply card (BRC). The card would be designed to grab the consumer's attention quickly before it hits the recycle bin or paper shredder. If successful, the card would then give the consumer the option of responding by returning the BRC, using a web page, a toll-free number, or another convenient method for the consumer to make contact. The printed piece must provide some type of incentive for the consumer to respond such as a discount of some type or a chance to win something. Another use for VDP might be in the form of a personalized brochure or booklet sent to the consumer after they have opted in using a web landing page or personalized URL.

It is important to understand that a personalized campaign may be targeted towards potential new customers or existing customers, or both. The campaign may be designed to sell something, or it may be designed to provide a service to existing loyal customers.

CAMPAIGN DEVELOPMENT

Developing a cross-media personalized marketing campaign should be done with great care. Personalized marketing can be very effective, but it can also be time-consuming and costly. It is important to work with a team of individuals that will ultimately be part of the campaign. This, of course, would include the client, or the person wanting to sell something; the marketer who may or may not be involved with other aspects such as data management; graphic design; and production. The marketer may have partnerships with others to do these tasks as well. The most likely clients for personalized campaigns will be clients who are willing to try new things and also have an adequate marketing budget. The most likely partners to work with will be those that have proven experience in personalized marketing. Since personalized marketing is still a relatively new concept, this can be challenging.

TRACKING AND ROI

One of the nice features of cross-media personalized marketing is the ability to track real numbers and calculate precise return on investments (ROI). Every email, every personalized URL, and every variable-data piece can be tracked by its own uniqueness. Responses can be measured, and those responses can be tracked to determine actual conversion rates. A ***conversion*** is simply someone who not only responds to a campaign but also performs the desired action. An ***action*** can be making a purchase or something else that the campaign was intended to do such as complete a survey, sign up for an event, or vote for something.

Tracking personalized marketing responses and actions and using that information to determine ROI can be time-consuming, but it is beneficial to show the client how effective the campaign was and how their marketing investment has paid off. The technology exists to effectively measure ROI so why not use that as a marketer's marketing tool.

THE FUTURE OF PERSONALIZED MARKETING

As this trend in personalized marketing continues, we'll continue to see creative ways of receiving marketing messages. Even now in the grocery stores, coupons will sometimes print on the back of your receipt based on your current buying habits. It won't be long before we'll see coupon holders in the isle flashing at us or talking to us because it recognizes our radio frequency identification (RFID) tag stored in our grocery store member card and it "knows" we might be interested in purchasing that particular item. It won't be long before we see other retail environments such as fast-food restaurants taking our order with a machine automatically and "remembering" what we ordered the last time because of our debit or credit card. You can bet we'll be offered special coupons to try and get us to buy that extra shake or piece of cheesecake.

ISSUES OF PRIVACY

Personalized marketing is unique to an individual. To most people, this is appealing. It breaks the stereotypical model of mass marketing. It gets closer to the consumer. This brings up the issue of consumer privacy.

How much information is too much to share with an individual consumer? Where do you cross the line between relevancy and an invasion of privacy? Many consumers are concerned about how much information is known about them. Caution should be used when developing a personalized campaign not to let consumers directly know how much you know about them. This can be very detrimental to a marketing campaign. Identity theft is an increasing reality with many consumers. More and more people are shredding their mail so they are less likely to become a victim of identity theft. Presumably, as we age our overall wealth increases. This means that as we get older we also may have more to lose.

With the use of the Internet and the culture developing from its use, consumers are becoming less sensitive about the information they share. Young adults today are Internet savvy and don't seem as reluctant to give information about themselves. They are creating blogs, posting pictures, and using email, instant messaging, and other forms of Internet activity to socialize with their peers. The fear of identity theft is still somewhat unknown to them.

It remains to be seen, however, what consumer trends will be with our society as our younger technologically savvy generations advance into a generation with more purchasing power. The digital era has changed so much of our society, and it is likely to continue creating a database culture where consumers will readily give up bits of information in exchange for some reward. This trend will continue to allow cross-media personalized marketing to grow. And VDP will remain a viable component of that process.

12. The Business of Digital Printing

STATIC VERSUS VDP

The business of digital printing and variable-data printing is a topic still in its development stages because of the shift occurring within the printing industry. It is important to differentiate between the business of static printing and VDP printing. The planning and production are quite different yet the digital printing engine is the driving technology that allows both to exist. Most digital printers today are finding that there is an increasing market for VDP, and most expect growth to continue in this area. Yet static digital printing still represents the majority of what is being produced on digital presses.

Most likely this trend will continue. VDP is just one component of digital printing. Static digital printing will continue to grow as it becomes more cost-effective to shift longer runs onto the digital presses. With any digital technology, the trend over time is generally for the costs to drop while the technology improves. This will also happen with digital presses as press manufacturers continue to remain competitive. Larger and faster models will be developed and the shift will continue towards more cost-effective printing on digital presses.

It is also important to understand the societal demands that will affect digital printing as well. As our society becomes faster paced, there is a fundamental shift for consumers wanting products now. Lead times typically required for traditional print production won't be acceptable as digital printing becomes more cost-effective. Look at the trends that have occurred in the consumer photography area as the shift has been made from analog to digital production. Leads times for consumers receiving their photos have gone from weeks, to days, to hours and even minutes. With digital cameras and photo printing options today, someone can take a picture and place it onto their own printer to make a high-quality instant photo.

The demand for fast turnaround times in static digital printing will continue. The length of runs that currently define "short run" printing will increase as press speeds increase and costs drop. The turnaround time for variable-data printing jobs will remain longer due to the increased complexity of the workflow. VDP jobs require more time for planning, creation, and implementation. Because of the uniqueness of VDP, the increased response rates, and the high-value customization unique to variable-data printing, there are greater opportunities for higher profit margins than in static digital printing.

BUSINESS MODEL

It is important to develop a business model that includes both static digital printing and VDP. If traditional printing presses are part of the current business model, they must also be incorporated into the new model. Planning becomes more critical than ever when digital printing is incorporated into the business model.

With traditional printing, production planning has become quite standardized. The time it takes to produce a job through the various areas of estimating/invoicing, design, prepress, press and postpress are quite predictable. Production schedules are created and profitable printers have learned how to adhere to the production schedule in the traditional printing environment. Production planning with digital printing can be an entirely different model, however. With digital printing the customer may want the job in hand in the time it takes to produce an estimate using traditional printing methods. By contrast, the majority of printers finds that the average sales cycle for VDP jobs are a month or longer and can sometimes be as long as a year. Planning for these various options can be challenging at best.

A good business model should include a good balance of the equipment usage and job variety for the most efficient production of existing equipment. Pricing and costing then need to be analyzed to balance well with production. In traditional printing the equipment capacity is generally at 85% or higher but this is harder to achieve with turnaround times inherent in static digital printing. A business model should include expected capacities closer to 50% to 70% for digital presses. This means that equipment costs and depreciation need to be spread over smaller monthly volumes for digital printing. VDP pricing, then, would need a different cost and pricing structure as the sales cycle will be even greater while still utilizing a digital press.

COSTING FOR DIGITAL PRINTING

Costing for digital printing involves giving an estimate to a customer and eventually pricing and invoicing the job. The hopes are that the estimate is the same or very close to the actual price of the job upon completion. If not, customers can be lost, profits won't be achieved, or both. It is important to re-evaluate the estimating process if this happens. Since estimating and pricing should be similar, they will be discussed similarly in this section as general costing. Digital printing has similarities but also differences to costing compared to traditional printing. Much can rely on the specific contract with a given press manufacturer. Most contracts include a ***click charge,*** which is essentially a licensing fee charged for each impression. The click charge can vary greatly depending on what is included in the fee. Some contracts have an all-inclusive click charge that would include the cost of things such as consumables, maintenance, and equipment depreciation. This click charge would presumably be on the high end of the pricing structure. Other structures can include a lower click charge but may not include any of the items previously mentioned.

If consumables are not included, paper costs and ink/toner costs must be determined. Often, the amount of coverage is factored in for use of ink/toner for a particular job. Waste is not as high for digital printing as it is for traditional printing because of longer makereadies associated with traditional printing. Still, waste should be factored into digital printing costs. If equipment maintenance and depreciation are not part of the click charge, they must also be factored into the overall costs. Finally, costs should also be considered for expenses such as building space, utility usage, and employee salaries.

Although estimating and pricing standards have been well established for traditional printing through the use of budgeted hourly rates (BHR) and activity-based costing, standard practices for digital printing have not been so clearly outlined. Most printers charge a price per piece for static digital printing. This makes it easier to do a direct comparison to any associated click charges inherent in digital printing costing structures. VDP does not lend itself well to such costing structures however.

Costing for VDP can be as customized as the job being produced. Because of this, developing a standard costing structure is difficult. Most printers selling VDP use one of the following methods for costing jobs:

- Cost per piece
- Cost per project
- Cost per response
- Cost per conversion

Cost per piece is the easiest method for billing, but generally not the best method for marketing and estimating. Often what will happen is a client will see that the cost per piece for VDP is higher than other printing methods and won't see the value of the personalized campaign. Marketing and selling VDP as a cost per project is the most common and logical method to use for costing as it allows the printer to calculate the overall cost by using a cost per piece if desired, but it also communicates to the customer what the investment dollars will be. Educating the customer using a cost-per-response scenario is a good idea, but can be risky if it is used for actual pricing.

If a digital printer really understands and believes in the effectiveness of VDP, they can enter into a true partnership with their client and cost a job based on the cost per conversion. A conversion is when the client achieves the desired results such as selling a product or getting someone to sign up for an event. If the printer is truly invested in the process and understands the benefits of VDP, this can be a good costing structure. For example, if a automobile company is selling cars as part of its VDP marketing campaign, the printer would get a percentage of each vehicle sold that was a direct result of the VDP campaign. As the ability to manage, control, and track data becomes perfected, this is a very reasonable method of pricing and could be the most profitable for the VDP printer.

MARKETING VDP

Full-color digital presses become one of the enabling technologies to creating and producing VDP. So naturally, one of the biggest marketers of VDP has been the digital press manufacturers. They have spent a great deal of time and money marketing to printers, their natural customers of the product they were selling. As printers began to invest in digital presses they then began to market VDP to their customers, most of whom didn't know what VDP was all about. Today, printers are still doing that through a variety of ways, including the following:

- Through a sales force experienced in selling commercial printing
- Through a sales force experienced in selling VDP
- Through direct mail pieces demonstrating VDP
- Through special seminars and meetings for prospective VDP customers

The logical people to market VDP to is the marketers. There has been more of a trend to do that and marketers are beginning to realize the value of VDP, especially as an entire personalized marketing campaign. Marketers are realizing, though, that not everyone is a good client for personalized marketing. Because personalized campaigns require more time and effort and are generally more costly, marketers are targeting companies that have higher marketing budgets or companies that are selling higher-valued items such as automobiles, electronics, or some type of service. As marketers begin to implement more personalized campaigns, that will drive the need for more VDP down to printers.

ROI AND VDP

Good planning and preparation for creating a business model and then developing good strategies for estimating and pricing will lead digital printers to an accurate return on investment. As trends can be analyzed and yearly volumes can be determined, the return on investment (ROI) can be easily measured. Another use for the term ROI is in the area of VDP and how to market jobs for VDP. Sales cycles are longer and costs are generally higher for VDP compared to traditional printing and static digital printing. But it is a well-known fact that VDP generates a higher response rate in marketing and generally translates to higher sales volumes.

ROI then must be demonstrated to consumers of VDP. This can be done through educating customers on VDP and the advantages associated with a VDP campaign. It is important to show a direct correlation between response rate and total project costs.

For example, table 12-1 represents a mailing of the same quantity but with different levels of targeting or personalization built into the campaign.

Table 12-1. Cost Analysis of a Mailing of the Same Quantity but Different Levels of Targeting or Personalization

	Non-Targeted Direct Mail	Targeted Direct Mail	Very Targeted Direct Mail
Quantity	20,000	20,000	20,000
Cost per piece	$0.33	$1.33	$3.33
No. of responses	200	1,600	5,400
Response rate	1%	8%	27%
Total project cost	$6,600	$26,600	$66,000
Cost per response	$33.00	$16.63	$12.33

The cost per response goes down as the direct mail piece becomes more targeted, but the overall project costs go up. The overall response rates go up as well. With good database selection and sorting, it is entirely possible that a list of perspective customers can be narrowed down in quantity to target only people who may be interested in a particular product or service. Table 12-2 shows the costs associated with a decreased quantity of mailings and the corresponding number of responses.

As can be shown, the overall project costs go up, but not proportionately to the increase in responses. Responses are 4 to 6 times higher as the campaign becomes more targeted, while the

Table 12-2. Cost Analysis of Decreased Quantity of Mailings and Corresponding Number of Responses

	Non-Targeted Direct Mail	Targeted Direct Mail	Very Targeted Direct Mail
Quantity	20,000	10,000	5,000
Cost per piece	$0.33	$1.33	$3.33
No. of responses	200	800	1,350
Response rate	1%	8%	27%
Total project cost	$6,600	$13,300	$16,650
Cost per response	$33.00	$16.63	$12.33

Table 12-3. Cost Analysis of Decreased Quantity of Mailings and 200 Total Responses

	Non-Targeted Direct Mail	Targeted Direct Mail	Very Targeted Direct Mail
Quantity	20,000	2,500	741
Cost per piece	$0.33	$1.33	$3.33
No. of responses	200	200	200
Response rate	1%	8%	27%
Total project cost	$6,600	$3,325	$2,468
Cost per response	$33.00	$16.63	$12.33

overall project costs are only 2 to 3 times higher. Table 12-3 shows yet another analysis of quantity changes. Let's say we are able to narrow our mailing list down even further to those we think may be interested in a product or service. With the same number of responses on each direct mail campaign, the overall project costs go down as the piece becomes more targeted. The response for each campaign is at 200 total responses, but the overall project costs go down from $6,600 to $3,325 to $2,468.

Once these types of numbers can be shown to VDP consumers, the ROI becomes much clearer. If ROI is to be taken a step further, response rates must then be compared to conversion rates. A conversion is simply a targeted individual acting on a desired action. The action might be to purchase a product, to sign up for an event, to visit a website or to respond to a survey. Since VDP is data-oriented by its very nature, this can be measured easily by tracking of responses and conversions.

Not all customers will want VDP campaigns to be tracked. But if it is desired, the responsibility of tracking and more accurately measuring ROI can be done by the marketing agency or by the digital printer.

MARKETING SEGMENTS

Business marketing segments. It is important for printers to understand who the clients are for digital printing and VDP. It is important to understand what business segments are represented by these clients. The more printers understand the consumers of digital printing, the better prepared they will be to market and sell to those segments. The Digital Printing Council has researched and published a series of three books (with accompanying CD-ROMs) entitled *Marketing4Digital*. The twenty-four marketing segments identified in this series of publications for digital printing are shown in table 12-4.

Table 12-4. Marketing Segments Covered in the *Marketing4Digital* Research Project

1. Advertising Agencies
2. Health Care (HMOs, Hospitals)
3. Cruise Industry (Hospitality and Tourism)
4. Department Stores (Retail Trade)
5. Gambling and Wagering (Casinos)
6. Automotive Industry (Manufacturers and Dealers)
7. Insurance
8. Real Estate (Brokerages)
9. Gas and Electric (Utilities)
10. Hotel (Hospitality and Tourism)
11. Office Supplies/Home Improvement (Retail Trade)
12. Banks (Financial Services)
13. Investment Companies (Financial Services)
14. Travel Agencies (Hospitality and Tourism)
15. Telecom (Utilities)
16. Professional Services (Legal, Accounting, etc)
17. Food Services—Wholesale
18. Food Services—Retail
19. Associations
20. Education (Public and Private Higher Education only)
21. Publishing (Magazine and Journal)
22. Pharmaceutical (Drug Manufacturers)
23. Religious Organizations/Philanthropy
24. Other

Job marketing segments. Job marketing segments for digital printing include short-run digital printing, custom publication printing, preprinted shells with VDP added using digital printing, VDP full digital printing, postpress VDP, transactional printing, versioning, and Web-to-print.

WHO IS INVOLVED?

The personnel involved in producing digital printing will vary greatly depending on whether it is static digital printing or VDP. As previously mentioned, there are vast differences between the two including the personnel involved in production from beginning to end.

There will be fewer people involved in preparing and producing static digital printing. The production workflow is similar to that of traditional printing methods. Content creation is usually done by a graphic designer, ad agency, or an end-user client. The digital file is then passed onto the digital printer. There may or may not be a prepress person involved. In digital printing, because the workflow is streamlined and makeready is significantly less, prepress may not be a necessary part of the workflow. A digital press operator will output the job on the digital press. If finishing and/or binding is needed, personnel in this area will also be involved.

VDP will likely involve an entire team of people including marketers, ad agencies, designers, data specialists, and the printer themselves. It is important when producing VDP to establish partnerships with the various personnel involved.

FUTURE TRENDS

We have already seen a natural progression of digital presses becoming more productive and this trend will continue. Consumable prices will also continue to decrease creating more demand for digital printing as it becomes more cost-affordable. Press manufacturers will continue to make presses that have larger sheet sizes and larger roll widths for both sheetfed and webfed digital presses. Although webfed presses tend to be capable of printing at higher speeds, there will still be a balance between both types of digital presses on the market. Since inkjet printing has shown tremendous growth in desktop and large-format printing areas, we can expect to see a growth in this area as well for digital presses.

Digital printing and VDP will continue to be growth areas. As more printers get into these areas, there will be opportunities for diversification into data and digital asset management, mailing, and fulfillment. Databases in particular are an area that is in need of ownership for updating and managing. Technical expertise is needed for managing personalized cross-media campaigns including VDP, email, and website management. Digital printers are a logical solution for clients in need of such services. Digital printers can provide an end-to-end solution for people looking for management of personalized marketing campaigns.

13. Digital Printing and the Plight of the Commercial Printer

The commercial printing industry segment is the largest in number of establishments with approximately 35,000 operations in the United States in 2006, most of which represents a prospect for digital printing. However, this number is substantially down from approximately 45,000 operations in 1996 and the number continues to decline. Yet this does not spell doom for the entire industry. Those companies declining in number are those that either have not accepted the fact that long-run "static" analog jobs are no longer the choice of many print buyers the way they used to be, do not understand or do not know how to integrate new technology into a traditional printing workflow, or are so over-capitalized with expensive traditional equipment that they do not have the investment dollars needed to modernize with equipment needed to serve the growing demand for digital short-run color and variable-data printing (VDP).

This chapter explores the plight of the commercial printer today in an era that is increasingly digital. It also explores what the digital equipment vendors need to know to successfully sell to this industry segment; they must first understand the culture of commercial printers and the present issues that they face.

Commercial printers are highly capitalized with traditional mechanical equipment and electronic equipment. They are used to large capital expenditures and carry a large debt. Many carry a debt at the maximum. They work on small margins: 2–2.5% after taxes. (Digital printer profits are often 2–3% higher than this.) The expected 2.2–3.4% growth over the past few years did not occur. It was more like 1.5% and is not expected to be any better in the foreseeable future. As the economy gains strength, the commercial printing segment will recover, but it is not going to be in the traditional realm of offset lithography but in the realm of digital printing.

Commercial printers are concerned about rapid obsolescence of highly electronic equipment (imagesetters, RIPs, scanners, front-end technology). The average traditional commercial printer is resistant to invest in automation for fear that new electronic and digital equipment will become obsolete before becoming profitable.

Commercial printers want the longest run possible in a market shifting to short runs. The traditional medium-to-large commercial printer believes that six- to eight-color offset presses are the answer to productivity and profitability. However, today the printer has to deal with shorter run lengths and faster turnaround times that are demanded by customers. There is also concern about cannibalizing long runs into smaller digital jobs. The commercial printer does not want to pull jobs off of large presses unless digital printing is less expensive.

Commercial printers base business sales on personal relationships over relatively long periods of time. Successful selling of digital printing requires spending a relatively short period of time with the account and then moving onto another account. This is unlike selling traditional long-run printing where the client is nurtured by the salesperson during and after the sale because the client is expected back for reruns and new jobs. These are very lucrative opportunities for many sales representatives. However, the commercial printer usually does not want to pay salespeople premium salaries and commissions as a motivator to sell digital jobs. Another concern is that customers typically come to the digital printer for one job and then want to use the same printer for others that the printer may not be well suited to handle.

Commercial printers come from a 500-year-plus culture with a craft undergirding. Traditional commercial printing companies typically involves mostly small companies that are family owned and have family employees. They tend to be in the $5 million to $10 million range and have been in business for 10 years or more. They presently face an aging workforce and have difficulty in finding competent, skilled employees.

Commercial printers speak a language specific to the industry and expects vendors to do the same. Examples of traditional commercial printing language include words such as hickeys, picking, scumming, tinting, dot gain, squeeze pressures, ink film thickness, fountain solution, blankets, work-and-turn, work-and-tumble, sheetwise, density, trapping, ghosting, ink strength, ink and water balance, roller stripes, form rollers, distributor rollers, perfecting, register, screen rulings, and many more.

Commercial printers understand a workflow that is over 500 years old. The average commercial printer does not understand digital workflow beyond imagesetters and computer-to-plate, and does not fully understand file management, data-based planning, and data-based management. The commercial printer typically uses traditional prepress people for digital front ends and does little coordination of files/applications with content creators/service bureaus.

Commercial printers manage by last-minute decisions and short-range planning. The traditional commercial printer heard about systems concepts for production but does not practice it. They often purchase systems but do not fully understand them, and they want the right answer immediately from vendors on how new systems can be made profitable in a short period of time.

With commercial printers, every detail about a print job influences price. Examples of detail that influence the price of commercial printing jobs are format, color, number of pages, quantity, inks, paper, press sizes, finishing, and so on. Digital printing introduces a host of other variables that commercial printers often do not understand. Some examples are data merging, file management, preflighting, "clicks," specialized paper and non-standard paper sizes, toner, inline finishing, and more.

Commercial printers sell based on cost per impression. The traditional commercial printer sells based on cost per impression or job and does not understand selling based on cost per response.

Commercial printers print what the customers want. The commercial printer does not intervene with what is best for the customer and simply prints what the customer wants. This is regardless if what is requested does not best serve the customers' marketing needs. The printer does not understand the advantages of becoming the customer's "creative partner," and not just a go-between.

Commercial printers see themselves as manufacturers rather than service providers. Commercial printing companies see themselves as manufacturers in the same sense as manufacturers that strive to produce the same product in exactly the same way from day to day, week to week, month to month, and year to year. An example would be an automobile manufacturer or food processor. There seems to be a failure in commercial printing to recognize that every print job is unique and that printing is "customized manufacturing." Nothing in commercial printing is "off-the-shelf," unlike other industries.

Commercial printers can do some maintenance on traditional/electronic equipment, but can't do any maintenance on highly electronic equipment. Traditional commercial printers understand electro/mechanics of presses with cylinders and rollers. They understand that fountain solution ("water") continues as a problem in lithography, and they typically know how to make needed adjustments to correct ink/water balance. However, they understand little about highly electronic digital equipment typified by today's technology. Hence, they must rely on expensive service contracts with equipment vendors as protection against problems that cannot be solved within the company. The insecurity about not being able to solve problems from within the printing company and the cost of service contracts inhibit commercial printers from developing markets requiring digital equipment.

Commercial printers rely on paper costs to inflate prices. As a buffer against waste and to protect small profit margins, commercial printers mark up the cost of paper and pass this cost onto customers. With the variability in the production of traditional printing jobs in prepress, press, and postpress, one error resulting in plate remakes or press reruns can mean the difference between a profit and loss on a printing job. The inflated paper prices passed onto the customer act as a buffer against costly errors in production. Additionally, traditional commercial printers are used to standard paper sizes. And, when problems occur on press, the tendency is to blame the paper first as paper is the most expensive disposable commodity in printing and yields the greatest return on claims when there are problems. There is insufficient focus on preventive maintenance where systems are set up in such a way and maintained to prevent problems from occurring.

Commercial printers are resistant to change and slow to change. Many commercial printers wish that there were not changes in technology to keep up with because such changes are tedious, expensive, require learning curves, and are not immediately profitable. Besides, they are confused about the "digital optimism" getting most of the "press" in the industry because they often do not understand how digital technology will better serve their existing client base.

Traditional equipment abounds in commercial printing. There is a large amount of traditional "iron" in the commercial printing industry, and the owners are looking to keep their investments solid. One commercial printer said, "I'd rather spend $1 million for a used Heidelberg press than $1 million for a new [digital/variable] press because three years from now, the Heidelberg will be worth close to that and the [digital/variable] will be worth a fraction of that."

Customers view printing as a necessary evil. Commercial printers deal with customers who see printing as a necessary evil and, therefore, want printing as soon as possible, at the lowest price, at the highest quality, and with no hassle. These are conditions often imposed when a customer must purchase something to be competitive but would prefer not making the purchase.

The predominant printing process of the commercial printer is offset lithography. The commercial printer understands the technology of offset lithography and can solve most on-press problems. Additionally, offset lithographic presses retain their value, and the printer's customers like the look and quality of offset lithography.

DIGITAL ON-DEMAND AND VARIABLE-DATA PRINTING

Digital on-demand and variable data printing is a different "animal." Providing the look and quality of offset lithography is its target. Not until this is achieved will digital printing substantially replace offset lithography as the dominant printing process for commercial printers. Some systems are coming close. Fundamentally, clients do not care whether their jobs are printed using conventional offset or digital printing. They care about the look of the final piece and about its cost.

VARIABLE-DATA DIGITAL PRINTING... IT'S ALL ABOUT THE BOTTOM LINE

Quality, speed, and low prices are what print buyers want, and they want it with no hassle on their end. The printer must present a logical case to the print buyers justifying the conversion from offset lithography to digital printing. Printers want technology from the equipment manufacturers that is trouble-free and easy to use. Hence, equipment manufacturers must make it comfortable for printers (who purchase the presses). Printers must make it comfortable for print buyers (who purchase printing as a disposable commodity). And, print buyers must make it comfortable for print consumers (who use printing for purchasing decisions).

Comfortable = Economics
Economics = Bottom Line
It's all about the bottom line

PROJECTIONS

The equipment manufacturers claim that in less than 10 years digital presses will double their pages per minute and have improved resolution. Those producing front-end systems claim that the next five years will show much needed simplified and better front-end production.

The 1980s and 1990s was the era of mass communication during which marketers wanted to blanket prospective customers with large volumes of the same marketing material. The printing industry responded by providing the technology to do this via larger and faster printing presses and data distribution systems through microwave relays and satellite transmission. This greatly expanded the direct-mail advertising industry, yet only resulted in an average response rate of approximately 2%. The twenty-first century, however, is the era of one-to-one direct communication during which marketers are learning that direct-mail response rates are vastly increased when each printed communication piece is personalized to suit the interests of the recipient.

While the technology to produce this personalized approach has been around for over 10 years, it was extremely expensive. More recently, the cost of digital variable-data printing has declined significantly, and this decline in cost is enlarging the market. The technology is getting better and faster each year. Color management has gotten less expensive and easier to implement, and better desktop computers, workstations, and RIPs have helped. Workflow has accelerated and throughput has increased. Overall performance has been dramatically increased.

On-demand printing was not a forethought of commercial printers five years ago but is now the fastest-growing segment in the industry with a projected annual growth rate of nearly 20%. All indications are that the future is specific, direct, one-to-one marketing, containing information based on good knowledge from a solid database. It is anticipated that by the end of the decade, there will still be printed books, but everything surrounding the book will change more than it has for the past 100 years. On-demand printing will soon become a routine service for a large percentage of commercial printers that make the transition. As a result, more titles will be in print, the sale of English-language titles will grow in non-English-speaking markets, and more non-English-language books will be sold in the English-speaking world. All this becomes increasingly possible and practical for the commercial printer because advances in color technology are improving reproducibility and consistency to a point where digital printing is encroaching on the capabilities of offset lithography

SURVIVING IN A CHANGING PRINT MARKET

How does the commercial printer survive in today's changing print market? The first step is to understand the concept of segmenting markets. There are two different markets that use traditional printing or digital variable-data printing. Traditional printing produces mass printing whereas digital variable-data printing produces personalized printing. Mass printing is typically purchased based on the lowest cost per piece. Yet, personalized printing costs substantially more and must not be sold on the basis of the lowest cost per piece or there would be no clients for it. Those who purchase printing must be educated, usually by the printer, to understand the concept of purchasing printing based on the cost per response before they will understand the value proposition behind variable-data printing. However, even before this, the printer must be educated to sell total marketing programs as opposed to individual jobs.

The concerns of the typical commercial printer used to attracting and selling the longest runs possible fall into two categories:

- If print buyers begin to understand the VDP value proposition, they will reduce the volume of work given to the traditional printer and move a portion of it to a variable-data printer.
- If VDP services become available at traditional commercial printing sites, the client will cannibalize long runs on a traditional four-, five-, or six-color press into much shorter runs on a digital press.

So, in some cases long runs will be cannibalized into shorter runs, but the traditional printer's oversight is that this adds value for the client and, hence, such cannibalization is inevitable as VDP becomes increasingly understood by those who purchase printing. Therefore, questions for the commercial printer to ask in determining whether to embrace or forego digital VDP include the following:

- Do they position themselves to keep the digital/variable printing within the confines of the company, or do they allow another printer to "steal" it?
- Do they re-establish their business model to allow for categorizing traditional and VDP printing, and allow long-run jobs to be broken into several variable-data short-run jobs in adding value to their customer's product?
- Are they willing to accept the notion that, should they forego providing the service of digital VDP, their longer-run jobs may be lost to short-run printers?

- Can they adjust their business plan and position VDP jobs to represent an additional product offering along with their standard longer-run jobs?

Some printers have reported that more than half of the jobs printed on digital equipment are for new applications rather than work migrating from traditional presses. Other companies successful in digital printing tend to have an existing client base or market niche that can benefit from higher-priced digital printing. It appears evident that as printers re-equip their plants for the future, difficult choices must be made between investments in conventional presses and emerging digital presses. Some industry analysts say that a mistake can put a firm's survival at risk. But failure to re-equip to meet client expectations for service and product value will almost certainly be fatal. With digital technology changing so rapidly, knowing when to harness new press technology has become one of management's most difficult tasks.

HARDSHIPS

For those delving into the world of VDP, there will be hardships. For printers dedicated to making the transition, the rationalization for the switch is obvious though painful. Variable-data digital printing is a hassle, particularly on learning and setting up front-end applications. Printing buyers are not used to VDP and have to spend a lot of time organizing databases and files. This is not something that printing customers want to spend time on. Additionally, printers have to establish skills in database management—something not part of the typical routine of the traditional printer. VDP jobs are complex and require a steep learning curve. Companies having trouble do not have the financial resources to put in digital processes, develop a market to fill that resource, and replace the technology in which they invested due to obsolescence in a short period of time. One printer invested in a VDP press only to discover that his customers did not understand or were not ready for VDP services. He wound up using the press as a conventional press and later replaced it with a digital, non-variable-data press that was more cost-effective.

For those inclined to make the move into digital on-demand and VDP, there are hardships that must be overcome. For example, technology changes and improves faster than traditional printers believe they can recoup their investment. Digital printing technology involves a high cost of acquiring the technology, has a short shelf life, and has little, if any, residual value. With a prevailing printing industry culture that is over 500 years old, printers have trouble making the change emotionally. This industry is typically afraid of change and the uncertainties connected with it.

One example of a major change in thinking involved is how the front end of the process is handled. A printer "going digital" has to increase hiring in data processing. A different skill set is needed than that of a designer or electronic prepress technician. For sophisticated variable-data jobs, the printer must invest a lot of time and money into front-end technology and personalization systems. There is a need for simplified front-end systems to handle variable data, and until such a need is fulfilled, highly trained specialists in data management will be needed to handle front-end applications to the digital printing press. The challenge of establishing, accessing, and maintaining good databases remains the top barrier for the growth of variable-data printing. The programming alone is a huge up-front investment, and the design, prepress, database management, binding, and inserting are all equally important to the total job.

The graphic arts industry has created good workflow for producing high-quality output for high-volume printing. However, it has not been sufficiently exposed to data management. The problem for the printer is to know how to merge mailing lists and images together, not merely responding to print buyers who hand over a job and asks how much it will cost.

TRADITION

As previously noted, tradition plays a role in the slow growth of short-run color digital presses and VDP presses. There is a large amount of traditional "iron" in the printing industry and the owners are looking to keep their investments solid.

It takes a different knowledge base and different kind of person to execute the VDP workflow relative to the traditional one. The printing industry and its customers, for the most part, are not ready to accept this radical change in understanding and application but will have to if the desire is to survive in the future. An example of an apparent denial that exists occurred at a printing industry conference conducted for content creators, advertising and marketing people, and print buyers. There was a panel presentation including someone representing each of the areas of prepress, press, finishing, and paper and ink suppliers. None of the panelists had much to say about digital variable-data printing. This was very telling. The entire panel spoke about traditional printing. When asked the question about the panel's position, observations, problems, and successes with variable-data digital printing, the moderator said, "I don't think that this is the right group to ask the question to." If not this group, then who?

In sum, average traditional commercial printers cannot afford to take the risk of the VDP investment required. They are not good at creating new ideas. They rely on sales representatives to sell on price, service, quality, and intangibles, as opposed to selling on cost per response and the value added by VDP. And they live by the standard sizes and ranges of paper typical of offset lithographic presses.

The difficulty of instituting on-demand and VDP printing, and selling the technology involved to the commercial printer, is that they come up against the prevailing publishing culture and cost systems of old print technology. This is all very difficult to break. However, the new paradigm offered by digital on-demand and VDP offers some attractive opportunities for printers. For example, the average per-unit production cost is the same, regardless of number of units ordered. Among the business unit's benefits is the ability to perform quick changeovers of between eight to ten minutes and require only a few seconds to reconfigure a job with no loss of "uptime." The value proposition offered by VDP shifts from providing print to furnishing tools to manage customer relationships with their clients. This is an entirely new way of thinking in establishing and nurturing customer relationships in the commercial printing industry.

The new paradigms of digital on-demand and VDP also includes digital/variable printing moving the printer from being a print provider to being a business communications services provider. It creates a new, integrated relationship with the customer, and the printer becomes a powerful alliance with the end-user community. Of course, cost per response becomes the key to color variable-data market penetration, and knowing what the printer's customer's customer is attempting to achieve (i.e., the customer's business objectives) must become part of the printer's business plan.

It is not that print is changing, it is that print's role in the media mix is changing, and this is stressing traditional industry relationships and calling into question the vision and business assumptions that have been the foundations of print business management for over 500 years.

For most printers, taking ownership of content is outside of their experience and skills. Hence, being a communications facilitator may be a better strategy for them; that is, offering mailing, e-marketing, shipping logistics, and other services that clients prefer to outsource.

Additionally, building ways of tracking and measuring end-user results becomes an important part of the printer's marketing plan. The more progressive printers may even consider expanding into a full marketing service provider and have authorized users customize brochures, letters, and sales materials, verify proofs, and submit orders through the Internet directly to the printer. In other words, the printer also maintains and manages the files for the printer's customers. It is anticipated that as VDP catches on, companies will demand that printed communication be as capable of customization as other forms of communication, such as web pages or email. It could turn out to be that the role of the printer becomes that of marketing communicator for the printer's accounts and handles these various multimedia communication tasks.

Much of this has to do with fulfillment. If the printer is handling a client's fulfillment, it can have a positive influence because it can also introduce digital applications for "responder" communications with the electronic channels that have been established.

MYTHS

Several myths prevail as rationalization for not pursuing VDP among skeptical printers. One myth is that VDP is a mini-niche market, and another is that it is a solution looking for a problem. Both myths are not fact-based. VDP is not a mini-niche market. It is a massive market that simply has not yet been tapped. It is not merely a local or national market. It is truly an international market. It is also not a solution looking for a problem. The prevailing direct-mail business market, in nearly all areas, faces tremendous problems in direct-mail returns of 2% or less when VDP has demonstrated that responses can approach the 20% to 30% range if implemented properly. Proper implementation means a good database, a good product or service, a well-designed mailing piece, and an efficient mailing/distribution system.

COMPETING FOR CUSTOMERS

As customers begin to realize the advantages and value added of VDP, traditional printers will either have to get into this business or figure out how they are going to keep their competitors from pilfering their customers. This is not a major issue today because most printer customers shun VDP for a number of reasons. Some claim that they do not have enough data about the recipient to justify variable, and printers often claim that their customers do not ask for digital variable-data printing. If anything, there is a preference to black variable data on the letters and reply devices for names and addresses only; a rather simple concept to understand. Many printing customers will not use four-color, variable-data brochures as the per-piece cost is too high and they have not yet accepted or understand the value of purchasing printing based on cost per response. Without a track record, the benefits of VDP are difficult to track, and without a history, it is difficult to place a value on customer retention. Additionally, files are complex and an impediment because buyers do not know how to prepare files. However, the entire matter is a bottom-line issue and price is a main barrier to widespread adoption of color variable-data printing. Print buyers are simply hung up on cost per impression rather than the results. They have not yet accepted that the decision to use VDP should not start with the cost per response. It should be started with the value of the result.

To begin overcoming this, some of the more progressive printers have begun educating their present and prospective customers through a series of "brown bag" luncheon seminars, evening receptions and talks, and plant tours. They usually focus on inviting marketing and advertising people to these events, as these are the people who are likely to understand the value of VDP.

Another effective approach is providing "mini" trial projects at little or no cost to the customer. This last approach is a good investment because it could be convincing. Once a VDP account is landed, it is typically a loyal account because the printer is often made privy to a confidential database, and clients do not like bouncing around from printer to printer with their client lists.

BUSINESS STRATEGY

One-to-one, personalization marketing has transpired over the past two years among Fortune 2000 companies. The demand for fast turnaround, quicker to market over competitors, and on-demand printing is up significantly over the last year, and turnaround speed is an essential feature required for success in today's business climate.

For digital on-demand and VDP printing to succeed (i.e., color digital printing), production costs have to come down, production speeds have to improve, and quality has to improve. In any event, if the client needs digital, it must be done to keep the business, and every part of the process must be streamlined to achieve the advantage of rapid turnaround speeds. Once production is streamlined, the focus must shift from production to other bottlenecks and particularly estimating, scheduling, planning, and order entry. Additionally, management must buy in to make the transition successful because nothing succeeds if the leaders do not believe it will work. Success in digital color printing depends on the commitment of upper management.

Those who sell digital printing technology also have an important role to play in developing successful strategies for printers. Digital and variable-data printing technology manufacturers are sometimes perceived to be more interested in selling hardware (boxes) than benefits. This needs to change. One strategy for equipment vendors is to hold periodic meetings with those influenced by digital printing. One meeting should be held for printing producers and another for print users. This could involve seminars at company sites during which printers are oriented on the most effective way of selling digital printing, and print users are educated on the benefits of short-run color, on-demand printing, and variable-data printing. Executives particularly must be educated on the possibilities of such non-traditional printing.

Obstacles in technology and fixed market mindsets must be resolved before the market for variable-data printing explodes. Getting to top executives may not be easy because they are not used to buying printing. Hence, the buying process and print-buying decisions must be related to bottom line advantages.

WHAT TO EXPECT—SOME PLUSES AND MINUSES

Those just entering the VDP arena can expect some negative and positive experiences. First, it will become quite clear early on that it is more expensive to produce sophisticated, well-planned, short-run variable-data pieces than traditionally printed pieces. Short runs mean increased administrative time. However, as digital variable-data work becomes less expensive to produce, as is expected in the future, more will buy it. Additionally, new, improved, and more efficient hardware and software will continue to drive the cost down. Today printers are finding that full-color, 100% variable capability presses are entering the production mainstream on an increasing basis as operating costs decline, as output quality improves, and as presses become wider and faster. While offset lithographic quality is clearly the aim of press manufacturers and the desire of printers and their customers, speeds and press sizes that approximate offset will increase the popularity of digital printing. However, until this occurs, digital on-demand and VDP will be a small part of the overall printing business. It will continue to be a hard sell for longer runs but logical for short-run color.

As previously noted, there are also cultural considerations that are inhibiting the printing industry's comfort with VDP. The industry practice is to separate content and intent from execution, and marketing VDP effectively requires combining these under the responsibility of the printer. Typically, the client or its advertising agency is responsible for content and the printer is responsible for execution. However, under the new VDP paradigm, while the printer may not create what the content says, manipulating, merging, and moving the content files are becoming the responsibility of the printer. Print-on-demand technology, for example, provides the answer to a publishing dilemma: how to get books to consumers where and when they want them. Where such delivery is traditionally the responsibility of the publisher, it is now becoming the job of the printer in providing total fulfillment.

So, what we see in digital on-demand and VDP is a compression of technology from the front end and the back end toward the center. Prepress has become integrated with press in the digital arena, and postpress including mailing and fulfillment has become the job of the printer in an integrated and sometimes closed-loop system. This addresses an age-old attitude of most companies that buy printing, particularly for advertising purposes, that printing is a necessary evil. It is something those who purchase printing wish that they did not have to spend money on but they must in order to remain competitive. It has already been noted that whenever something is viewed as a necessary evil, the buyer wants it at the lowest price, at the highest quality, as fast as possible, and with the least hassle and time spent on it. Full-color digital printing is positioned to address these needs once the pricing, quality, and speed issues are addressed, and they will be. Advances in color technology, combined with a higher demand for short-run color, on an on-demand basis, presents an unfolding profit center for newcomers who are not strapped with capitalization and debt related to traditional technology as the black-and-white market reaches maturity.

MOTIVATING SALES

Selling on-demand and VDP differs from selling traditional printing. Selling traditional printing is typically based on developing long-term relationships with accounts and pursuing long runs that generate lucrative commissions for printing salespeople. This requires nurturing accounts during and after the jobs have been completed. A successful salesperson selling traditional printing can make a long-term living on only a handful of accounts. On the other hand, selling on-demand or VDP involves pursuing many accounts desiring relatively short runs. So what the salesperson must do is land an account, turn it over to the printer's customer service representative, and then move onto landing the next account. There is no time for the nurturing process, nor does the salesperson see value in nurturing because the commissions on individual short-run jobs are low. It is much more difficult to sell on-demand and VDP. To attract salespeople wanting to do this, there must be financial incentives such as higher-than-average salaries and relatively high commissions. In a traditional commission system, salespeople make more money selling offset printing because of the time it takes to develop a variable imaging account. Some sales salaries range from commission only at 10% of gross sales to $2,500 per month plus a 10% commission. One printer reported paying salespeople $10 to $20 per hour plus 3% commission after achieving gross monthly sales of $40,000. Another reported paying $25 per hour including a commission.

Added to the difficulty of selling VDP is the fact that most printing sales representatives do not understand the value proposition behind variable-data printing, and this makes it hard for them to be consultative to their clients. It takes a talented, well-educated salesperson to sell variable imaging. Again, the problem solution is in the compensation package. The qualified digital/variable salesperson needs a high base salary, a bonus for gaining an account (any size), and a variable amount tied to eventual sales. Qualified digital/variable sales representatives are rare because they have to know how to sell to marketers who do not want printing, but wants leads. The ability to help customers generate leads is a key part of the sale. In some cases new sales staff are added to traditional printers getting into VDP. In other cases new compensation packages are created as an incentive for those selling traditional printing to also sell VDP. However, regardless of who is selling the product, VDP is more difficult to sell and more expensive to produce than traditional direct-mail pieces. It is a "difficult sell" because it is a much more sophisticated process, and most printers work with print buyers who buy on price alone with no consideration given to cost per response or that VDP is a program that delivers a better return on investment.

Even those highly successful in selling digital printing find that variable data is a "difficult sell" compared to offset because variable imaging suffers from insufficient knowledge on the part of traditional marketing departments and business executives. They do not understand it but they eventually will. It is a matter of time before those selling via direct-mail advertising begin to realize that the advantage is in variable data's increased relevance to the recipient. This realization is speeded when the printing salesperson focuses selling the VDP concept to marketing and creative people as opposed to production staff and those who merely buy printing. One printing company executive said, "We spent the first year in business convincing people that there was a market and that this was a worthwhile venture."

Some suggest that, in digital on-demand and VDP, it is not the strongest that survive. It is those who adapt to change who survive. But finally, it is the bottom line that tells the story. For example, divide the cost of a traditional, non-variable, offset print project by the number of leads it generates, and do the same for the digital variable-data job. This is a convincing value proposition to sell VDP: a significant reduction in the price of what the customer wants—responses.

SUMMATION

The future of the printing industry relies on the growth of digital printing and particularly variable-data printing. Static commercial printing is declining each year and has been for the last decade. One-to-one marketing, i.e., personalized printing, the focus of VDP, has been established as an application worth pursuing because of the personal appeal of such communication, and the relatively high response rate that results. Personal communication is nearly always more effective than impersonal communication. The commercial printers that survive in the future will be those that embrace the concepts of digital and variable-data printing. They will have abandoned the notion that long-run static printing is the key to profits and come to realize that an entirely new business model has emerged that defines success in commercial printing, particularly for the small to middle size printer.

Glossary

ablation. Method of imaging digital proofs or CTP plates by vaporizing small amounts of material, typically with a thermal laser. Also refers to the process of writing data to optical memory with a laser that burns holes into thin metal film.

action. In a marketing campaign, getting a person to perform a desired activity, such as making a purchase. See also *conversion.*

address correction requested. An endorsement that authorizes the USPS (United States Postal Service) or CPC (Canada Post Corporation) a fee to provide the new address, when known, of a person no longer at the address on the mailing piece.

Adobe Acrobat. A software program that allows users to read portable document format (PDF) files, which are electronic versions of printed documents that maintain the attributes (bold and italic type and other formatting choices) assigned to a printed original. See also: *portable document format.*

Adobe Acrobat Distiller. A software application that converts PostScript language page descriptions into PDF files.

aliasing. A jagged or "staircase" effect in a raster image, caused by an insufficient number of image samples.

American Standard Code for Information Interchange (ASCII). A standard code that uses a set of seven-bit coded characters (eight bits when the parity check is included) to facilitate information interchange without formatting codes among data processing, data communications systems, and associated equipment. The ASCII set consists of both control and graphic characters.

antialiasing. The process of averaging between pixels of different colors, in order to produce a smoother, more blended transition between the edge of two areas rather than a distinctly jagged, staircase effect.

antivirus program. The essential software that detects and destroys rogue applications designed to damage a computer.

AppleTalk. A local-area network standard for Macintosh computers.

application program. The computer software designed to perform actual jobs as opposed to the system programs that manage equipment operation.

applications program interface (API). Systems software that allows computer programmers to create interface features or, in a network, determine how the various features will be used.

archive. A group of compressed files.

archival storage. The long-term storage of image information on photographic, magnetic, or other media.

artifact. A visible defect in an electronic image, caused by limitations in the reproduction process (hardware or software). An aliasing patterns (a jagged or "staircase" effect in a raster image) is an example of an artifact.

ASCII file. A text file containing no special formatting, containing only those characters defined by the American Standard Code for Information Interchange. The lowest common denominator for exchanging text among programs. Almost any word processor or desktop publishing program can read or write ASCII files. Also known as *text-only files.*

background processing. Procedure by which a computer can execute one function, such as printing, while the user simultaneously executes another function, such as word processing or image editing.

backgrounding. In electrophotography, an uneven print that can occur due to a bad or worn doctor blade/bar, improperly charged toner particles, or wrong-signed toner particles.

backup. The act of saving information on a computer system to tape or disk for safekeeping.

banding. In digital output, a defect in a gradient (color blend) in which the discrete steps (shades) of the gradient are visible; usually produced when the system or output device cannot generate enough gray or color levels to render a smooth gradient.

bandwidth. A frequency measurement expressed in cycles per second (hertz) or bits per second (bps) of the amount of information that can flow through a channel.

baud rate. The speed of information transfer between electronic devices expressed in data bits per second or the maximum number of changes that can occur per second in an electrical circuit. Baud is often used interchangeably with bits per second but this is incorrect.

bezier curve. A vector graphic, named after Pierre Bezier, that is defined mathematically by two endpoints and two or more other points that control its shape.

binary digit (bit). See *bit.*

binary file. Information stored as binary digits; in other words, in machine-readable form. Images transported over the Internet are encoded as binary files.

binding. Joining the assembled pages of a printed piece together. Binding takes many forms including saddle-stitching, adhesive binding, mechanical binding, loose-leaf binding, and Smyth sewing.

bit. A binary digit—the smallest unit of information used in a computer file. It has one of two possible values—zero or one—used to indicate "on" or "off" or "yes" or "no" in the storage and transfer of electronic information and images. See also *byte.*

bitmap. An image represented by an array of picture elements (pixels), each of which is encoded as or more binary digits.

bits per second (bps). The speed at which data is transferred over a computer modem and telephone line.

bleed. A printed image (pictures, lines, or solid colors) that extends beyond one or more of the finished page margins so that when the paper is trimmed, the image "bleeds" off the edge of the sheet

block. A specified quantity of logical records stored together between inter-record gaps, constituting a physical record.

bus. A pathway for transferring data among several devices, located between two end points with transmission restricted to one device at a time. Also the interconnection of a series of computer processors.

bus topology. A local-area network (LAN) configuration, such as Ethernet, that requires all of the network terminals to be linked by a single backbone cable with signal terminators at each end. See also *local area network.*

byte. A single group of bits (most often eight) that are processed as a unit. Also the smallest addressable unit of main storage in a computer system. See also *bit.*

carrier beads. In electrophotography, magnetic materials that are specially coated with a polymeric film to provide the proper triboelectric properties for attracting and transporting toner.

CFF/Type 2 (Compact Font Format). A font format specification developed by Adobe. that occupies less storage space than Type 1 fonts. Storage space usage is lowered by using operators with multiple arguments, various pre-defined default values, more efficient allotment of encoding values and shared subroutines among FontSet (family of fonts). OpenType fonts can also contain glyph outlines in a CFF table.

charge generating layer (CGL). On an organic photoconductor drum, the layer that consists primarily of a semiconducting organic chemical that releases electrons (allowing current to flow) when exposed to light.

charge transport layer (CTL). The outer layer of an organic photoconductor drum. In addition to its role in image formation, it protects the surface of the drum from wearing down to the the CGL.

cleaning blade. See *wiper blade.*

cleansing. In database management, the process of removing duplicate information, bad records, incomplete records, or errant characters. This can be done manually or automatically with some type of cleansing software or simple scripts that can be incorporated into the database.

click charge. A fee that the digital printer or digital press manufacturer charges the user of the equipment, usually based on the number of impressions per month. The click charge is often associated with a method of financing the purchase or rental of the equipment.

cluster selection. A selection routine based upon taking a group of names in series, skipping a group, taking another group, etc. For example, a cluster selection on an *N*th name basis might be the first 10 out of every 100 or the first 125 out of 175, etc.; a cluster selection using limited postal code might be the first 200 names in each of the specified postal codes, etc.

CMYK. Abbreviation for cyan, magenta, yellow, and key (black), the four printing process colors or inks used to simulate full-color printing.

cold offset. A ghost image picked up in the fuser.

color gamut. The range of colors that can be formed by all possible combinations of the colorants in a color reproduction system.

color management system (CMS). A set of computer programs or utilities that are used to ensure color calibration by accurately translating from one color space to another throughout the production process. A CMS ensures consistent color throughout the prepress and print processes by calibrating the color relationships among the scanners, monitors, printers, imagesetters, proofers, and other devices in the chain from input to output, usually creating a device profile for each device. Color management consists of three primary steps: (1) calibration of input devices, monitors, and output devices to known specifications, (2) characterization, which is a way of determining the color "profile" of a particular device, and (3) conversion, which performs the "color correction" function between color-imaging devices.

color match. Condition resulting when no significant difference in hue, saturation, and lightness can be detected between two color samples viewed under standard illumination.

color swatch. A small, printed solid used for color matching or measurement. It represents what an ink color might look like after it is printed.

compiled list. Names and addresses derived from directories, newspapers, public records, tradeshow registrations, etc., that identify groups of people via a common link.

compression. A software or hardware process that reduces the size of images so that they occupy less storage space and can be transmitted faster and easier. This process is accomplished by removing the bits that define blank spaces and other redundant data, and replacing them with a smaller algorithm that represents the removed bits. Data must be decompressed before it can be used.

computer-to-plate technology. Those imaging systems that receive fully paginated materials electronically from computers and expose this information to plates in platesetters or imagesetters without creating film intermediates.

Configurable PostScript Interpreter (CPSI). A PostScript interpreter that can be set up—configured—to read PostScript code and convert it to raster data to generate output for specific output devices, such as imagesetters, color proofers, laser printers, high-speed printers, large-format imagesetters and plotters, and direct-to-plate devices. CPSI can thus be modified to drive a complete range of devices within a single company's line of PostScript products.

content creator. The person who generates the actual information contained by a document, presentation, web page, etc., independent of the structure, layout, and design. The content creator can be the client or person desiring the finished product, a graphic designer, a prepress provider, an ad agency, or some type of marketing personnel.

content management. Processes involved in organizing, categorizing, and structuring information resources so that they can be stored, published, and reused in multiple ways. A content management system can collect, manage, and publish content, storing the content either as components or whole documents, while maintaining the "connections" between components.

continuous-feed printer. Production machine that is fed nonstop by a roll of paper and can cut each printed piece to size. CF printers offer the industry's fastest print speeds, around 1,000 images per minute.

continuous inkjet (CIJ). An output technology in which drops of ink are generated in a stream and deflected through a plate to the substrate.

continuous tone. A photographic image or art (such as a wash drawing) that has not been screened. It has infinite tone gradations between the lightest highlights and the deepest shadows.

conversion. (1) In marketing, getting a person to take action, whether it be providing more information or making a purchase. (2) Translating a color image from the color space of one device to that of another. Also known as color transformation.

copy, hard. Printed machine output of a photographic proof or text.

copy, soft. Text or images viewed or previewed on a video display terminal. See also *proof, soft.*

cracking (at the fold). An aesthetic defect that can occur when paper is folded against the grain if the paper fibers (or paper) actually break.

cross-media personalized marketing. A form of personalized marketing that incorporates various media in getting the message to the customer.

customized marketing. See *personalized marketing.*

customized printing. See *variable-data printing.*

cyan. A blue-green color, complementary to red. Along with yellow and magenta, one of the three primary subtractive colors, or process colors used in the printing process. Cyan reflects blue and green light, while absorbing red.

data. Text, audio, video, and images stored in a form the can be understood by a computer.

data compression. See *compression.*

data conversion. Technique of changing digital information from its original code so that it can be recorded by an electronic device using a different code. Data created in one software format may be converted to another before printing. Data must also be converted for various output devices, such as when RGB colors are converted to CMYK.

data mining. In database management, the extraction of implicit, previously unknown, and potentially useful information from data.

data transfer rate. The sustained speed at which data can be written or read and conveyed by a device, generally given in kilobytes per second (KBps) or megabytes per second (MBps).

data transmission. In computing, the sending of computer information—such as a file—over a network or other form of telecommunications link.

database. A collection of information about a particular topic, such as sales or billing. It is organized to facilitate ease of retrieval and analysis.

database server. A computer that uses a specialized process to manage the database itself. Most work with relational databases and are based on a client/server architecture.

decompress. The process of returning compressed data to its original size and condition.

desktop. The space in a computer represented on the display screen (as in a Macintosh environment) by document, folder, file drawer, printer icons, etc. The electronic equivalent of an office desk, it is used to create, edit, and store documents.

desktop publishing. The creation of fully composed pages with all text and graphics in place on a system that includes a personal computer with a color monitor; word processing, page-makeup, illustration, and other off-the-shelf software; digitized type fonts; a laser printer; and other peripherals, such a scanner.

DI®. Trademarked acronym for Presstek's direct-imaging system.

dialog box. Window appearing on a computer screen requiring the user to provide additional information before a command can be completed or to choose among different options.

dial-up connectivity. Linking to a computer network via modem and regular telephone lines.

digital. Method of representing information in numerical (binary) code. Unlike analog signals, digital signals have only two states: either "on" or "off."

digital asset management (DAM). The process of storing, retrieving, and distributing digital assets (files), such as logos, photos, marketing collateral, documents, and multimedia files in a centralized and systematically organized system, allowing for the quick and efficient storage, retrieval, and reuse of the digital files that are essential to all businesses.

digital copier. Machine that integrates scanning and printing functionality to perform the copy function. Unlike an analog (light-lens) copier, it creates an electronic representation of the image.

digital front end (DFE). A multifunctional system that connects and outputs to the print engine or the digital press itself. A typical DFE can rasterize (rip) file, impose documents, color-manage files, archive files, and implement variable-data printing.

digital press. A machine that outputs images digitally (e.g, via electrophotographic means) and designed to handle high-volume production-level printing (i.e., output speeds of 70 ppm or faster). Compared to an offset lithographic press, a digital press can produce short-run jobs more economically, integrate with the Internet, and incorporate variable data.

digital printing. Any output process that does not use a fixed-image and consumable image carrier (a plate) and that creates an image from digital data. Images are placed on a substrate through the use of spots or dots using a toner, inkjet, dye or pigment-based transfer system.

digital transmission. A communications mode in which the data to be transferred is represented as discrete (and discontinuous) electronic pulses or signals, the values of which are stored as a series of zeros and ones, otherwise known as binary digits.

digitize. To convert an image or signal into binary form.

direct-imaging press. A printing press in which the printing plates are imaged directly on the press—using digital data—rather than away from the press, as when a separate platesetter is used.

direct-to-plate technology. See *computer-to-plate technology.*

distribute-and-print. A workflow in which digital files are created at a source location and then distributed to multiple locations where digital presses at each location print smaller quantities. The alternative to this workflow would be to print larger quantities of the job at a single location and then ship the printed job to various locations.

distributed printing. Printing directly to printers and/or digital presses that are located far from the operator's workstation. May include multiple destinations for a single job. Often associated with on-demand and short-run printing.

doctor blade/bar. Located between the magnetic roller and the toner hopper, this device regulates how much toner is fed from the toner hopper to the magnetic roller. Too little laser toner results in a light print, while too much laser toner can cause excessively dark prints and possibly leakage. Alternative term: *metering blade/bar.*

dot. (1) The individual element of a halftone; it may be square, elliptical, or a variety of other shapes. (2) The individual spots of output from a marking engine.

dots per inch (dpi). A measure of the output resolution of a device. The higher the number, the sharper the type and images.

download. To transfer a file or files from a remote computer to a local computer's hard drive.

driver. A software program that controls a specific hardware device such as a scanner or printer.

drop-on-demand (DOD) inkjet. A nonimpact printing method in which ink droplets are emitted only when required for imaging—i.e., the digital signal stream is in the "on" mode.

drum. See *organic photoconductor (OPC).*

duplicate (dupe). In database management, two or more name and address records that are found to be equal under the list user's basis of comparison (match code, mathematical formula, etc.). Essentially, it is a record that matches another record. There are different kinds of duplicates. Personal dupes are the same person at the same address. Household dupes are different people at the same address.

dye sublimation. A imaging process that utilizes a sublimable dye imprinted on a carrier sheet to transfer images to a receiving sheet by placing them in direct contact with each other.

dynamic layout software. Software for variable-data printing that allows the form and content to be separate and that automatically adjusts the layout to accommodate varying sizes of graphics and text fields.

dynamic printing. A category of printing in which the image on the image carrier must be re-generated for each page. This facilitates variable-data printing. See also *variable-data printing; static printing.*

ElectroInk. A patented liquid toner used with the HP Indigo series of digital presses.

electronic data interchange (EDI). A standard for the exchange of business documents, such as invoices and purchase orders.

Electronic mail (email). Messages sent from computer-to-computer.

electrophotographic digital press. A digital output device that uses electrophotography (xerography) as its imaging principle and operates at production-level speeds (i.e., 70 ppm or faster).

electrophotography. Processes (including xerography and laser printing) that produce images by passing toner particles over an intermediate photoconductor drum, which receives an electrical charge that enables it to transfer the toner particles to plain (untreated) paper, forming the image

electrostatic printing. See *electrophotography.*

encapsulated PostScript (EPS). A device-independent graphics file format that stores the images not only as a series of Bezier curves (or vectors), but also includes a low-resolution bitmap representation of the file for quick on-screen viewing.

encrypt. To convert data into such a form that it cannot be read if intercepted by the wrong people. Only those who hold the key to an individualized encryption scheme can decrypt these messages.

enterprise system software. Specialized software applications that are primarily code-based and are used exclusively within a particular company or business. This category of software tends to be robust and can be largely responsible for digitally managing virtually everything within an organization.

EPS. See *encapsulated PostScript.*

Ethernet. A local area network (LAN) architecture, originally designed by Xerox, that transmits data throughout a network at 10 Mbps using the carrier sense multiple access/collision detection (CSMA/CD) access protocol. A newer version of Ethernet, called *100Base-T* (or *Fast Ethernet),* supports data transfer rates of 100 Mbps. The newest version, *Gigabit Ethernet* supports data rates of 1 gigabit (1,000 megabits) per second.

explicit personalization. The use of personalization in such a manner that the targeted recipient is acutely aware that the message has been personalized for him or her because it contains text or images specific to the given individual such as that person's name or business address.

Extended Binary Coded Decimal Interchange Code (EBCDIC). An eight-bit configuration used to represent up to 256 separate characters (alpha, numeric, and special characters). EBCDIC uses the eighth bit as an information bit, which differs from ASCII, which uses one of the eight for parity.

Extensible Markup Language (XML). A general-purpose markup language for creating special-purpose markup languages, capable of describing many different kinds of data. Its primary purpose is to facilitate the sharing of data across different systems, particularly systems connected via the Internet.

extension. A three-letter suffix added to file names to indicate the software application that created the file.

field. A segment of a record that contains specific information. In a database, fields should contain the same information for each record. For example, all name fields should contain a name, all postal code fields should contain a postal code, etc.

file layout. A way of laying out or formatting list information in a computer file that puts every piece of data in a specific position relative to every other piece of data and limits the amount of space assigned to that data. If any data is missing from an individual record or if its assigned space is not used completely, that space is not filled. Every record has the same space and the same length. Any data exceeding its assigned space limitation must be abbreviated, contracted, or truncated. See also *record layout.*

file server. A workstation primarily responsible for redirecting resources across the network. Dedicated file servers require that the computer running the server software not be used for other tasks. Nondedicated servers permit the administrative tasks and the shared resources to be spread over various network nodes.

file transfer protocol (FTP). The tool used to retrieve information in the form of electronic files from any number of computer systems linked via the TCP/IP protocol. Users in effect transfer copies of information found on remote computers either directly to their own computers or to a service provider's network and then to their own computers.

finishing. All forms of completing graphic arts production, including folding, trimming, and assembling sections; binding by sewing; wire stitching; gluing; and diecutting or gold stamping.

firewall. The layer of security that protects internal computer networks from outside intrusions, particularly from the Internet.

fixed-length field. In a database, a field with a set limit to the number of characters.

fixing assembly. See *fuser.*

flat model. A type of database consisting of a single, two-dimensional array of data elements usually containing rows and columns.

folding dummy. A mockup of a press sheet that shows the placement of page heads, the binding edge, and the gripper and side-guide edges, as well as page sequence and signature arrangement.

font. A complete collection of characters in one typeface and size, including all letters, figures, symbols, and punctuation marks.

four-color process printing. The photomechanical reproduction of multicolor images achieved by overprinting specified amounts and areas of yellow, magenta, cyan, and black inks.

fuser. In electrophotography, the device that uses a high-temperature heating element to cause the toner to adhere to itself and the paper. Alternative term: *fixing assembly.*

GIF. See graphics interchange format.

gigabit (Gb). 1,024 megabits.

gigabyte (GB). 1,024 megabytes.

grain direction. In papermaking, the alignment of cellulose fibers in the direction of web travel. In printing, paper is *grain-long* if the grain direction parallels the long dimension of the paper and *grain-short* if it parallels the short dimension. Paper folds better in the grain direction.

gradient. Any smooth progression from one color or gray value to another, usually comprising a series of steps that, ideally, should be imperceptible. Often used as a background.

graphical user interface (GUI). A visual way to represent computer commands and objects on screen. The user interacts with the computer by selecting icons and menu items from the screen, usually by moving and clicking with a mouse.

graphics. Artwork, photographs, and charts that are reproduced or presented in visual form.

graphics interchange format (GIF). The most common method of encoding and storing picture files on the Internet's World Wide Web. It was originally developed by Unisys for use on CompuServe specifically for compressing photographic images online.

hairline. The thinnest line that can be reproduced by an output device.

halftone. A printed reproduction that simulates a continuous-tone image by using dots that vary in frequency (number per square inch), size, or density, thereby producing tonal gradations.

hertz. A unit of measurement of electrical vibrations in cycles per second.

host. A computer that functions as the beginning and end point of data transfers.

hot offset. A ghost image picked up in the fuser.

house list (house file). Any list of names owned by a company as a result of inquiry, buyer action, or specific targeting (usually with research).

hyperlink. An emphasized word or phrase that connects related documents in a hypertext system.

hypertext markup language (HTML). The hypertext document format used on the World Wide Web.

hypertext transfer protocol (HTTP). The Internet standard supporting the exchange of information on the World Wide Web.

illustration program. A program used to create object-oriented graphics.

image personalization application. An application for variable-data printing that allows personalized or variable information to be incorporated directly into an image. The graphic image would be saved and then incorporated into a VDP layout as a variable image.

impact printer. An output device that uses mechanical striking elements to produce hard copy. The typewriter is an example of an impact printer.

imposition. The process of assembling pages in the proper orientation so when folded and cut, the pages come out in sequential order.

indicia. Permit information for the post office as printed on a "self-mailer" brochure, magazine, or label.

ink trapping. How efficiently one ink film lays down on the preceding ink film when printing multiple colors. Compare with *trapping.*

inkjet digital press. A digital output device that uses inkjet technology as its imaging principle and operates at production-level speeds (i.e., 70 ppm or faster).

inkjet printing. A nonimpact printing process in which a stream of electrostatically charged microscopic ink droplets are projected onto a substrate at a high velocity from a pressurized system. The electrically controlled flow of droplets is either intermittent or continuous.

input resolution. The resolution (density of pixels) at which a scanner captures image information, measured in pixels per inch (ppi).

Internet. The "official" name for an international network of computer networks linked to provide and share information and resources about a seemingly limitless number of topics. The Internet, as we know it today, grew out of an effort formulated by the United States government in the late 1960s to protect the important data stored on its computers and to ensure the continued electronic transport of this data in the event of a nuclear war.

Java™. A programming language that enables developers to write small applications including animation and other advanced features that can be downloaded and run very quickly with most Internet browsers.

Job Definition Format (JDF). An industry standard designed to simplify information exchange between different applications and systems in and around the graphic arts industry. It enables the integration of commercial and planning applications into the technical workflow.

Joint Photographic Experts Group (JPEG). The compression scheme based on the discrete cosine transform (DCT) lossy compression algorithm that is a de facto standard on the Internet. As developed by the Joint Photographic Experts Group in collaboration with the International Standards Organization (ISO) and the Consultative Committee for International Telegraphy and Telephony (CCITT), JPEG allows the user to control the compression ratio and reproduction quality at the point of compression. It can also incorporate other algorithms, such as one-dimensional modified Huffman compression for lossless compression.

kilobit (Kb). 1,024 bits.

kilobyte (KB). 1,024 bytes.

laser. A high-energy, coherent (single-wavelength) light source. The small spot of light produced by the laser is used to expose light-sensitive and photoconductive materials at high speed and high resolution.

laser printer. A type of output device that utilizes electrophotography and a laser to print toner-based images on the paper. The laser recreates the image on a negatively charged drum which will then collect toner that is positively charged to attract to the areas of the image. The paper is then negatively charged; therefore, the positively charged toner is attracted to the paper and then is fused onto the paper.

laser printing. Process that uses lasers to create the image on a print drum, or photoreceptor. Areas on the drum hit by the laser attract toner. The printer transfers the toner from the drum to the paper and fuses the toner in place with heat.

Laserwriter, Apple. The first desktop laser printer to contain PostScript, introduced in 1985 by Apple.

latent image. The invisible image on the surface of an organic photoconductor (OPC) drum after exposure to light but before the application of toner to the surface of the drum.

light-emitting diode (LED). A semiconductor diode that emits light when subjected to an applied voltage and that is used in digital displays. LEDs are also used to expose photosensitive film, paper, or plates in some imaging devices.

line art. A drawing with no grays or middletones. Traditionally, black lines on white paper.

lines per inch (lpi). The unit of measure that designates the resolution of a halftone screen. Screens with a higher number, such as 120 or 133, have a higher resolution than screens with lower numbers, such as 65 lines per inch. See also *screen frequency*.

liquid toner. In electrophotography, a category of toner that uses a solvent instead of carrier beads, which makes the toner a liquid instead of a solid. See also *ElectroInk*.

list broker. A specialist who makes all necessary arrangements for one company to use the list(s) of other company(s). A broker's services may include most or all of the following: research, selection, recommendation, and subsequent evaluation.

lithography. A printing process in which the image carrier is chemically treated so that the nonimage areas are receptive to water (i.e., dampening or fountain solution) and repel ink while the image areas are receptive to ink and repel water. The image carrier is said to be planographic, or flat and smooth.

local area network (LAN). A group of interconnected computers linked over a relatively small geographic area that allows several people at the same business site to access the same set of documents. See also *network.*

lossless compression. An image compression scheme that uses a mathematical formula to infer the likely value of a pixel based on the the values of surrounding pixels. Because lossless compression algorithms do not discard any of the data, the decompressed image is identical to the original.

lossy compression. An image compression scheme that uses a mathematical formula to remove data that is the least perceptible to the eye. This improves the speed of data transfer but causes a slight degradation in the decompressed image.

magenta. The subtractive transparent primary color that should reflect blue and red and absorb green light. It is one of the four inks used in process-color printing.

mail merge. The earliest form of variable-data printing which allowed a database file of names and addresses to be merged with a Microsoft Word file, thus producing a "personalized" form letter.

makeready. All of the operations necessary to get the press ready to print a job.

marking engine. The heart of the digital press. The device responsible for physically placing the marks, usually dots, on a page. Marking engines image dots based on the particular technology of the digital press—e.g, a dot of dry toner or liquid toner, or an inkjet dot. See also *raster image processor.*

mass marketing. The process of widely marketing a product to the masses, using one or more of the mass media—radio, television/cable, Internet, newspapers/magazines, and signage (billboards).

megabit (Mb). 1,024 kilobits.

megabyte (MB). 1,024 kilobytes.

megahertz (MHz). One million hertz.

merge/purge. In database management, the process, usually aided with software, of analyzing certain parts of records to determine whether two records are duplicates and eliminates one of the records.

metering blade/bar. See *doctor blade/bar.*

microfine toner. Toner particles that average 8 microns or less in size.

mining. See *data mining.*

misregister. Printed images that are incorrectly positioned, either in reference to each other or to the sheet's edges.

modeling. In database management, the process of using data attributes to build profiles of potential buyers.

moiré. An undesirable, unintended interference pattern caused by the out-of-register overlap of two or more regular patterns such as dots or lines. In process-color printing, screen angles are selected to minimize this pattern. If the angles are not correct, an objectionable effect may be produced.

monochrome. Any image that comprises a single color, although it is most often used to refer to a black-and-white image.

Moore's Law. Developed by Gordon Moore, a law stating that computing power doubles every 18 months.

mopier. Contraction of "multiple original printer."

Multiple Master fonts. A font-rendering technology developed by Adobe Systems that can reproduce the characteristics of almost any typeface.

native format. The default file format used by a specific software application. A native file format is proprietary, and these types of files are not generally meant to be transferred to other applications.

network. A computer system that allows several users at remote terminals to exchange data electronically through a common central computer. See also *local area network.*

network interface card (NIC). The device that links one workstation to another in a network.

node. Any device capable of identifying itself on a computer network.

nonimpact printer. An output device that produces hard copy without the use of mechanical striking elements or the use of a permanent image carrier.

object linking and embedding (OLE). A Microsoft standard for creating dynamic links between documents that can be updated automatically. OLE is also used to embed a document created in one application within another application. It is incorporated into both Windows and Macintosh system software.

object-oriented. Graphic images created with mathematical descriptions, in terms of x-y coordinates instead of the pixels found in a bitmap. Object-oriented graphics can usually be displayed or printed at the full resolution of the monitor or output device, offering more precision than bitmapped images.

offset. See *lithography.*

on-demand printing. Commercial-quality printing produced as needed with turnarounds of a few hours or less. Often associated with very short runs of a hundred or fewer pieces and the use of a digital printing press.

on-demand publishing. The printing of a book that is done entirely through a digital process that makes it possible to print any number of copies at a given time. With traditional printing, involving a typesetting process, it was necessary to produce relatively large quantities of a book to get the price down to where it could be sold through the retail channel. With on-demand printing, it is possible to produce short-runs of books at a cost that still enables sales through the retail channel and to libraries.

one-to-one marketing. See *personalized marketing.*

one-to-one printing. See *variable-data printing.*

online. The state of a computer being connected to and communicating with another electronic device.

open. Readily accessible. In reference to standards and specifications, refers to the interoperability and ease of data exchange among different products or services from different vendors and intended for widespread adoption. Compare with *proprietary.*

open prepress interface (OPI). A set of standardized protocols that allows desktop equipment to be linked with color electronic prepress systems (CEPS). High-resolution color images are stored on a central network server, and low-resolution files are used for positioning, scaling, etc. in the page-layout program. At output time, the high-resolution images are swapped for the low-resolution images.

open-system color. A system of color reproduction in which input and output devices are characterized using device-independent color space, allowing color matching among multiple devices.

Open Type fonts. A cross-platform font file format developed jointly by Adobe and Microsoft in which bitmap, outline, and metric data are combined into a file, simplifying font management.

operating system. The master program that a computer needs to start up and perform basic tasks. It allows the computer to control itself and perform other functions, such as managing memory allocation for application software and data files.

organic photoconductor (OPC). A cylinder or belt coated with a substance whose magnetic properties change in the presence of light. The drum is magnetically charged and the laser changes the charge on the parts of the drum it passes over. Those areas will pick up toner and apply it to the page.

orientation. The direction in which a page is printed, i.e., the portrait (vertical) or landscape (horizontal) mode.

original equipment manufacturer. A producer who sells goods to another company for use as components in their own equipment or for resale to end-users. An OEM may sell only to companies for resale or may also compete in the end-user marketplace.

output device. Any machine—such as a laser printer, imagesetter, or phototypesetter—that translates the electrical impulses representing data as processed by a computer into permanent results.

output resolution. The quantity or density of dots that an a given output device, such as a laser printer, is capable of producing. It is measured in dots per inch (dpi). The higher the output resolution, the smoother the appearance of text or graphics.

page-description language (PDL). In an electronic publishing system, the format by which all of the elements to be placed on the page, their x-y coordinates (respective position on the page), and the page's position within the larger document are identified in a manner that the output device can understand.

page layout. The process of positioning art, types, rules, photos, running heads, etc. into the proper position on a page, originally accomplished by manually adhering each element to a "board" ready for camera work and now accomplished using specialized computer software.

page-layout program. A specialized computer program that allows the user to position type and other image elements automatically so that fully paginated electronic output can be generated.

PageMaker. The first "desktop publishing"(page-layout) software developed by Aldus in 1985 for the Apple Macintosh computer.

pages per minute (ppm). The output speed of a printer's marking engine as rated by the manufacturer.

paint program. A program used to create bitmapped graphics.

parsing. To separate or take apart. In database enrichment, the process of looking at parts of the file to make sure things like the field names are correct and the data has delimiters in place and in the correct fields.

personalized marketing. A form of targeted marketing—i.e., sending a specific message to a specific person—that uses interactive media such as the Internet, personalized web pages, and personalized emails. Personalized marketing is a four-phase process: identifying potential customers; determining their needs and their lifetime value to the company; interact with customers so as to learn about them; and customize products, services, and communications to individual customers.

Personalized Print Markup Language (PPML). An open, interoperable, device-independent XML-based industry standard printer language for variable-data printing defined by a group called the Print On Demand initiative (PODi).

Personalized Print Markup Language/Variable Data Exchange (PPML/VDX). A open variable-data exchange standard that combines the benefits of both PDF and PPML technology. A combination of PPML version 2.1 and PDF version 1.4, it allows for open data exchange across individuals, vendors, and platforms.

personalized printing. Printing designed to be unique for one specific person and includes variations of text, graphics, and layout to meet the needs of the individual consumer. Personalized printing, a type of variable-data printing, means that each page is distinctly different from the other. See also *variable-data printing.*

personalized web page. On a website, a customized landing page designed/created for a single individual.

photoreceptor. Physical device inside a marking system on which the latent image is written by a laser or LED bar and then developed with toner.

pixel. Picture element. The smallest tonal element in a digital imaging or display system.

pixelization. (1) A technique used to represent areas of complex detail as relatively large square or rectangular blocks of discrete, uniform colors or tones. (2) An undesirable condition of digital images in which the individual pixels are large enough to be egregiously visible.

pixels per inch (ppi). The input resolution at which a scanner captures image information.

plate. A thin metal, plastic, or paper sheet that serves as the image carrier in many printing processes.

platesetter. An electronic device that images printing plates directly from digital data on a drum or flatbed using a laser or other imaging technology.

plug-and-play. The ability of a computer to detect and configure a new piece of hardware automatically, without the user having to reconfigure the hardware elements.

plug-in. A software utility developed to operate through another application, performing a specific task.

plug-in application. A variable-data printing application that works in conjunction with an existing program (such as a page-layout program) to assist in incorporating and merging the data into the static elements.

point. The smallest American unit of typographic linear measurement, equal to 0.0138 in. Type height is measured in points.

portable document format (PDF). A computer file format that preserves a printed or electronic document's original layout, type fonts, and graphics as one unit for electronic transfer and viewing. The recipient uses compatible "reader" software to access and even print the PDF file. See also *Adobe Acrobat.*

positive image ghosting. In electrophotography, the problem of toner adhering to any latent image remaining on the OPC drum if the corona wire fails to completely recharge the drum during the conditioning or charging step of the process.

POSTNET barcode. A barcode developed by the United States Postal Service (USPS) to encode zip code information on letter mail for rapid and reliable sorting by barcode sorters. The POSTNET barcode can represent a five-digit zip code (32 bars), a nine-digit ZIP+4 code (52 bars), or an eleven-digit delivery point code (62 bars).

PostScript. A page-description language (PDL) developed by Adobe Systems used to output documents on laser printers and other types of devices, such as imagesetters. Considered the *de facto* output standard for desktop publishing, PostScript is an object-oriented language, meaning that it treats images, including fonts, as collections of geometrical objects rather than as bitmaps.

PostScript, encapsulated. See *encapsulated PostScript (EPS).*

preflighting. An orderly procedure using a checklist to verify that all components of an electronic file are present and correct prior to submitting the document for high-resolution output.

prepress. All printing operations prior to presswork, such as design and layout, typesetting, graphic arts photography, image assembly, and platemaking.

preprinted shell. A color "shell" of static information, normally printed by traditional printing methods such as lithography, that is then run through a digital output device to add black-only varying elements to the preprinted piece. This can be a cost-effective method to generate a full-color variable-data piece when only black is required for the varying elements.

primary charge roller (PCR). A roller in an electrophotographic output device (e.g., laser printer) that places the primary charge on the drum and erases any residual charge from the previous pass.

print engine. See *marking engine.*

Printer Control Language (PCL). A set of printer commands, developed by Hewlett-Packard, that provides access to printer features.

printer driver. Software that serves as the communication link between applications and the page-description language used by printers.

printer's spread. A pair of pages in the order necessary for printing, folding, and binding to yield the desired results.

process colors. The three subtractive primary colors used in printing (cyan, magenta, and yellow, plus black).

proof. A prototype of the printed job made photomechanically from plates (a press proof), photochemically from film and dyes, or digitally from electronic data (prepress proofs). Prepress proofs serve as samples for the customer and guides for the press operators. Press proofs are approved by the customer and/or plant supervisor before the actual pressrun.

proof, soft. An intangible image, such as that on a video screen, that is viewed for the purpose of approval.

proprietary. Privately owned and controlled; e.g., a language or format developed by a particular company for use with its own hardware or software and not readily available to all vendors. Compare with *open.*

protocol. A structured set of rules.

random-access memory (RAM). Solid-state computer memory that is essentially the "working" memory a computer uses to store temporary information. RAM can be read from and written to, as the name indicates, in a random sequence, and it is used to store data from open applications as well as the operating system itself.

raster. An image composed of a set of horizontal scan lines that are formed sequentially by writing each line following the previous line, particularly on a television screen or computer monitor. See also *bitmap.*

raster file. An electronic file in which the pixels are scanned and input in rows.

raster graphics. The representation of images as a matrix of individual pixels (dots), each with their own color or tonal value.

raster image processor (RIP). The hardware and software configuration used with output devices to translate data from PostScript and other high-level languages into dots or pixels and to determine the value and location of each dot or pixel. See also *marking engine.*

rasterization. The process of converting a vector-based or other image into a bitmap.

reader's spread. A pair of pages positioned across the binding edge, or gutter, from each other after the book is assembled; e.g., pages 20 and 21 of a book.

read-only memory (ROM). Nonerasable, permanently programmed computer memory. It can be accessed and "read" by the user but it cannot be edited.

record. A collection of related data or words treated as one unit.

record layout. A written, field-by-field description of the data contained in a record, typically describing each field as to its length, beginning and ending positions, name, editing characteristics and data format (i.e., character, hex packed, etc.). See also *file layout.*

relational model. A type of database that contains multiple tables similar to the one table created by a flat model but the tables can relate to each other and be linked through a key field.

resolution. (1) The quantity of dots or pixels on a page or display. The higher the resolution, the smoother the appearance of text or graphics. Input resolution is measured in pixels per inch (ppi), and output resolution is measured in dots per inch (dpi). (2) The precision with which an optical, photographic, or photomechanical system can render visual image detail. Resolution is a measure of image sharpness or the performance of an optical system. It is expressed in lines per inch or lines per millimeter.

RGB. The color space of red, green, and blue. These are the primary colors of light, which computers use to display on the monitor. Graphic images are usually captured by digital camera or scanner in additive RGB color mode.

rich black. An enchanced, deep black consisting of 100% black and tints of one or more of the process colors. One rich black might consist of 100% black, 50% cyan, 40% magenta, and 40% yellow. Another might be 100% black and 30% cyan. Alternative term: *super black.*

run-length encoding. A system of encoding digital data to reduce the amount of storage needed to hold the data without any loss of information. Each coded item consists of a data value and the number of adjacent pixels with the data value. This is a very efficient way of encoding large areas of flat color as used in linework and text.

sampling rate. The amount, as expressed in inches or millimeters, of electronic information sampled in both scan directions.

sans serif. Typeface designs, such as Helvetica, that lack the small extensions on the ascenders and descenders referred to as serifs. See also: serif.

schema. The structural description of records or facts in a database and the relationship between them.

scoring. A finishing operation that involves impressing a hard metal rule into the paper surface where a fold is to be made. This creates a cleaner fold on heavy, hard-to-fold paper or paper with a tendency to crack.

screen angle. The position of the rows of dots on halftone screens in relation to a reference grid with horizontal and vertical lines. The most dominant color screened is positioned at a 45° angle to the reference grid.

screen frequency. A measurement equaling the number of lines or dots per inch (lpi) on a halftone screen. The higher the screen ruling, the greater the detail in the halftone. Screen rulings range from only a few per inch for large billboards to over 200 lpi for high-quality printing on coated paper. Alternative term: *screen ruling.*

segmented marketing. Compared to mass marketing, a method of marketing in which a smaller group of recipients are identified and sent a more specific message based on their demographics.

self-extracting file. A compressed file that includes an executable program that causes it to decompress, usually by double-clicking. A self-extracting archive (SEA) is a group of self-extracting files.

serif. The short, usually perpendicular line found at the end of the unconnected or finishing stroke of a character. Serifs may vary in weight, length, and shape and contribute greatly to the style of the typeface. See also *sans serif.*

server. A device on a computer network that allows networked users (clients) access to a specific service on the network. An example is a file server, which allows the users to share data files and application software.

service bureau. (1) a company that provides imagesetter output of digital files; (2) a company that processes, cleans, zip code sorts, and otherwise manipulates a data file.

service provider. A business that specializes in Internet and LAN/WAN network connectivity.

sheetfed press. A printing press that feeds and prints on individual sheets of paper (or another substrate). Some sheetfed presses employ a rollfed system in which rolls of paper are cut into sheets before they enter the feeder; however, most forward individual sheets directly to the feeder.

short-run printing. Generally considered the printing of quantities less than 5,000.

signature. A printed and folded sheet of paper that results in multiple pages in the proper order for a publication. Signatures are usually in page sets of 4, 8, 16, or 32 pages.

small computer systems interface (SCSI). A computer port used to link the machine with external peripherals.

software. The stored instructions (programs) that initiate the various functions of a computer (the hardware). Instructions may be written in machine language or in another programming language, then compiled, interpreted, or assembled into machine language. Word processing, page-layout, and drawing programs are a few of the software programs used in the graphic arts. There are also other more specialized software programs that control high-end color electronic prepress systems and even some presswork applications.

sort. A processing function that arranges the contents of a file in a specified sequence.

specification. (1) A detailed description of the requirements for a job. (2) A step on the path towards formal standardization, but can be incomplete and is inherently subject to change and development. Conformance to a specification allows a degree of standardization in advance of the development and formal ratification of a standard; input in the specification development process by commercial organizations can help ensure the longevity of resources produced in conformance with these specifications.

spot color. The use of one or more extra colors (in addition to cyan, magenta, yellow, and black) on a page, used for a number of purposes including highlighting specified page elements.

spread. An image that extends across two facing pages in a book or magazine, crossing over the binding. See also *reader's spread* and *printer's spread.*

stand-alone application. A self-contained variable-data printing application that allows for the import of either an EPS or PDF for static elements and that allows variable information to added within the program.

standard. A detailed, formally ratified and fixed technology, format, or method that enables the performance of a particular task or activity. Compare with *specification.*

static printing. A category of printing that uses an image carrier with a fixed image. An example would be offset lithography, which prints from a printing plate. See also *dynamic printing.*

static text. Text that contains no variable information, it will not change when browsing through the database.

static web page. On a website, a landing page designed to attract a group of people. It can be used as a marketing tool to gather information from individual visitors or an option for a company to design and generate VDP.

stochastic screening. A halftoning method that creates the illusion of tones by varying the number (frequency) of micro-sized dots (spots) in a small area. Unlike conventional halftoning, the spots are not positioned in a grid-like pattern. Instead, the placement of each spot is determined as a result of a complex algorithm that statistically evaluates and distributes spots under a fixed set of parameters. With first-order stochastic screening, only the number of dots in an area varies, but with second-order stochastic screening, both the number and size vary. Alternative term: *FM screening.*

Structured Query Language (SQL). The most popular computer language used to create, modify, retrieve, and manipulate data from relational database management systems. The language, an ANSI/ISO standard, has evolved beyond its original purpose to support object-relational database management systems.

subsample. The process of recording and saving regular, nonconsecutive bits of data.

super black. See *rich black.*

tagged image file format (TIFF). A file format for exchanging bit-mapped images (usually scans) between applications.

telecommunications. (1) The transmission of data and/or voice over the network of telephone lines. (2) Any data transmission from one independent device to another, regardless of distance or method.

thermal wax transfer. A technology used in many color printers in which a waxlike ink is transferred to the page as a series of dots using a heat process.

tire tracks. In electrophotography, wavy lines running down the page, often associated with a worn doctor blade.

toner. (1) A type of very concentrated pigment or dye used in printing inks to alter the color strength of an ink. (2) A fine powder—"dry ink"—that can hold an electrostatic charge and used to create an image in electrophotography, such as in laser printers and photocopiers. It is made either mechanically (pulverizing ingredients into tiny particles) or chemically (growing ingredients from the molecular level into tiny particles of a precise shape and size).

total ink coverage (TIC). The total buildup of ink on a given spot on the paper; i.e., the sum of the percentages of black, cyan, magenta, and yellow printing at that spot. Printing processes have limits on the maximum TIC, somewhere in the 250% to 300% range. Alternative term: *total area coverage (TAC).*

transactional printing. The production of large volumes of documents from data and information in databases, using systems that dynamically merge data with electronic forms, such as statements, invoices, checks, and insurance policies.

Transmission Control Protocol/Internet Protocol (TCP/IP). The system that monitors and performs data transfer over the Internet. TCP sends data and IP receives it. On individual computers TCP/IP is the software component that enables users to access the graphical aspect of the World Wide Web.

transparent personalization. The use of personalization in such a manner that the targeted recipient is not aware that the message has been personalized for him or her.

trapping. The creation of a slight overlap between the background and foreground colors to compensate for the inevitable misregister that occurs in a printing process. Trapping helps to avoid a white space between two adjoining colors or generating a noticeable third color if misregister is excessive. Alternative term: *image trapping*. Compare with *ink trapping*.

triboelectric charge. A friction-induced static charge between two dissimilar materials.

trim size. The final dimensions of a page.

TrueType™ fonts. A type of computer font format created by Apple Computer as an alternative to Adobe PostScript fonts. TrueType fonts can be used both for bitmapped screen display and for vector-based output, the goal being to eliminate the need for two sets of fonts: screen fonts and printer fonts.

truncate. To drop characters at the end of a data field because the field being converted or keyed in is too long to fit in the record position in which it must be stored.

Type 1 fonts. A variety of PostScript font developed by Adobe Systems that includes in its font description special hinting algorithms that make them more quickly rendered, more compact in file size, and more appealing aesthetically.

type family. A set of typefaces derived from one basic design, e.g., the bold, italic, and condensed variations of the original face.

typeface. A distinctive type design, usually produced in a range of sizes (fonts) and variations, including bold and italic.

uniform resource locator (URL). The World Wide Web address of a company, service, or other information resource.

Universal Printer Pre and Post-Processing Interface (UP3I). An open specification that allows for a wide variety of devices to interface together, regardless of the manufacturer.

universal serial bus (USB). A standard for interconnecting peripheral devices with a computer that provides a wider bandwidth than that of a conventional serial bus or the Apple desktop bus (ADB).

UNIX. The computer environment in which the Internet has been and continues to be developed. It is used to run powerful workstations and networks where multitasking and multiuser access is essential. UNIX is also the parent operating system of DOS, which, in turn, spawned the Windows operating systems prevalent on PCs today.

upload. To transmit a file from a local computer's hard drive to the hard drive of a remote computer.

utilities. A set of computer routines, used primarily for system maintenance or to facilitate applications, such as copying to disks, creating directories, or searching for information.

variable-data printing (VDP). A form of on-demand printing in which elements (such as text, graphics, photographs, etc.) can be changed from one printed piece to the next, without stopping or slowing down the press, using information from a database. For example, a set of personalized letters, each with the same basic layout, can be printed with a different name and address on each letter.

variable-length field. In a database, a field with an adjustable length; the length of the field is stored within the field

vector file. An electronic file that describes geometric shapes and dimensions in terms of coordinates or other symbols.

vector graphics. The use of geometrical primitives such as points, lines, curves, and polygons, which are all based upon mathematical equations, to represent an image.

vectors. Mathematical descriptions of images and their placement.

versioning. A printed piece that has been customized in some manner for the local market but not the specific recipient, such as including a regional toll-free number or listing the address of the local hardware store or home improvement center.

vignette. A halftone, drawing, or engraved illustration in which the background gradually fades away from the principal subject until it finally blends into the nonimage areas of the print

webfed press. A printing press that prints on a continuous roll of paper instead of individual sheets.

web-to-print application. Software that allows the creation of VDP jobs by using a website to put together the elements.

wiper blade. The device that removes the untransferred toner from the surface of the OPC drum so that it can be recharged and used again. Alternative term: *cleaning blade.*

wiper blade flip. A problem that occurs when the edge of the wiper blade flips upward, due to a poorly lubricated blade. It is usually indicated by a thin vertical line on the page.

workflow. In a production environment, all the stages that a project or job must page through until it is completed. At its simplest, it is the movement of documents and/or tasks through a work process. More specifically, workflow is the operational aspect of a work procedure: how tasks are structured, who performs them, what their relative order is, how they are synchronized, how information flows to support the tasks, and how tasks are being tracked.

workstation. A full-featured computer that is used for work production and is connected to a network. It is typically dedicated to use by one person.

workstation-based application. A category of variable-data printing application that runs completely on a computer workstation. The static and variable images are planned and assembled on the workstation. Workstation-based applications can be further categorized into the following: image personalization, stand-alone, plug-in, dynamic layout, and enterprise system.

World Wide Web (WWW). A hypertext program that allows users to access related documents across global networks by navigating a series of electronic links. Developed by scientists at CERN, the European Particle Physics Laboratory in Geneva, Switzerland, in 1989, the WWW was originally text-based. Introduction of the graphical browser NCSA Mosaic in 1993 made it possible to access the color imagery, sound, and video that we commonly associate with the WWW today.

xerography. Technology invented by Chester Carlson in 1938 that started the copying revolution and gave birth to Xerox Corporation. An original image is transferred when light is projected onto an electrically charged surface. The image attracts oppositely charged toner particles, which are then fused into place on the copy paper, reproducing the original image. The word "xerography" is derived from the Greek words for "dry" and "writing."

Index

About the Authors

Dr. Penny K. Bennett is an Associate Professor in the Graphic Communication Department of California Polytechnic State University in San Luis Obispo, California. She teaches in the areas of electronic publishing, digital prepress/printing, consumer packaging, and specialty printing. Dr. Bennett has a Ph.D. in Education from the University of Idaho. Her Master's degree is from University of Nevada, Las Vegas, and her Bachelor's degree is from Ferris State University in Big Rapids, Michigan.

Her areas of expertise are in file creation and preparation for successful output, workflow and output issues, packaging, prepress, and VDP/digital printing. Dr. Bennett has written publications in the areas of Web-based instruction, expanded gamut printing, PDF, and digital and variable-data printing. She has been a presenter at a variety of conferences nationally including FFTA Forum, GRAPH EXPO/ PRINT trade shows, and the IPA conference, as well as at international conferences in Mexico, Puerto Rico, and Russia. She is also a member of and actively involved in several organizations including Printing Industries of America, Ghent PDF Workgroup, Foundation of Flexographic Technical Association, and Accrediting Council for Collegiate Graphic Communications.

Dr. Bennett also participates in conducting seminars and workshops through Cal Poly's Graphic Communication Institute. She has also conducted research in the areas of web-based instruction, multichannel media, variable-data printing, and cross-media personalized marketing. Dr. Bennett has also done consulting in her areas of expertise. She presently resides in San Luis Obispo, California.

Dr. Harvey Robert Levenson is a Professor and Department Head of Graphic Communication at California Polytechnic State University in San Luis Obispo, California. His teaching and research specialties are printing, technology, communication, media, and research methods. Dr. Levenson holds four degrees in printing and communication including a Ph.D. in Rhetoric and Communication from the University of Pittsburgh. Over the years, he has actively served on committees and boards of many graphic arts organizations including GATF, the Technical Association of the

Graphic Arts (TAGA), Electronic Document Systems Foundation (EDSF), and the Graphic Arts Literacy Alliance (GALA). He is presently president of ACCGC. Dr. Levenson is an active researcher, consultant, and speaker on matters related to printing, technology, graphic arts patents, media, and communication, and he has authored many articles and books on these subjects. He has been a technical consultant to approximately 250 printing and related companies. Dr. Levenson's latest books are *Understanding Graphic Communication: Selected Readings* (published by Printing Industries Press) and *Some Ideas About Doing Research in Graphic Communication* and *Introduction to Graphic Communication* (published by The Good Neighbor Press). Born and raised in Brooklyn, New York, he presently resides in Atascadero, California.

Frank J. Romano has had a career in the printing and publishing industries spanning over 40 years. Many know him best as the editor of the International Paper *Pocket Pal* or have read one of the hundreds of articles he has written for publications from North America to Europe to the Middle East to Asia and Australia. He is the author of over 44 books, including the 10,000-term *Encyclopedia of Graphic Communications* (with Richard Romano), the standard reference in the field. He has authored most of the books on digital printing. He has founded eight publications, serving as publisher or editor for *TypeWorld* now *Electronic Publishing* which ended with its thirtieth year of publication, *Computer Artist, Color Publishing, The Typographer, EP&P,* and both the *NCPA* and *PrintRIT Journals.* His columns appear monthly in the *Digital Printing Report.* He is the editor of the *EDSF Report.*

He lectures extensively, having addressed virtually every club, association, group, and professional organization at one time or another. He is one of the foremost keynote speakers. He has consulted for major corporations, publishers, government, and other users of digital printing and publishing technology. He wrote the first report on on-demand digital printing in 1980 and ran the first conference on the subject in 1985. He has conceptualized many of the workflow and applications techniques of the industry and was the principal researcher on the landmark EDSF study, "Printing in the Age of the Web and Beyond." He continues to teach courses at RIT and other universities and works with students on unique research projects.

About Printing Industries of America

Printing Industries of America, along with its affiliates, delivers products and services that enhance the growth, efficiency, and profitability of its members and the industry through advocacy, education, research, and technical information.

Printing Industries of America developed from the 1999 merger of the Graphic Arts Technical Foundation (GATF), founded in 1924, and Printing Industries of America (PIA), founded in 1887. This consolidation brought together two powerful partners: the world's largest graphic arts trade association representing an industry with more than 1 million employees and $156 billion in sales and a nonprofit, technical, scientific, and educational organization dedicated to the advancement of the graphic communications industries worldwide.

Printing Industries of America's staff of researchers, educators, and technical specialists helps members in more than 80 countries maintain their competitive edge by increasing productivity, print quality, process control, and environmental compliance and by implementing new techniques and technologies.

In addition to striving to advance a global graphic communications community through conferences, Internet symposia, workshops, consulting, technical support, laboratory services, and publications, Printing Industries of America promotes programs, services, and an environment that helps its members operate profitably.

Many of Printing Industries' members are commercial printers, allied graphic arts firms such as electronic imaging companies, equipment manufacturers, and suppliers. Its special industry groups, sections, and councils were developed to serve the unique needs of specific segments of the print and graphic communications industries and provide members with current information on their specific segment, helping them to meet the business challenges of a constantly changing environment. These groups focus on web offset printing, label printing, binding, financial executives, sales and marketing executives, and digital printing.

Printing Industries Press publishes books on nearly every aspect of the field; training curricula; audiovisuals and CD-ROMs; and research and technology reports. It also publishes *Printing Industries of America: The Magazine,* providing articles on industry technologies, trends, business management practices, economics, benchmarks, forecasts, legislative and regulatory affairs, human and industrial relations issues, sales, marketing, customer service techniques, and management resources. The magazine represents the consolidation of *GATFWorld* and *Management Portfolio,* formerly bi-monthly publications of the association.

For more information about Printing Industries of America, special industry groups, sections, products, and services, visit www.printing.org.